Brand Storytelling in the Digital Age

S M A Moin

Brand Storytelling in the Digital Age

Theories, Practice and Application

palgrave
macmillan

S M A Moin
Coventry University London
London, UK

ISBN 978-3-030-59084-0 ISBN 978-3-030-59085-7 (eBook)
https://doi.org/10.1007/978-3-030-59085-7

This Palgrave Macmillan imprint is published by the registered company Springer Nature Switzerland AG
The registered company address is: Gewerbestrasse 11, 6330 Cham, Switzerland

This book is dedicated to Professor James Devlin and Professor Sally McKechnie for they have taught me how seeking knowledge can change a life.

Foreword

In the context of evolving digital transformation and proliferation of social media in all aspects of life, the marketing game is changing. Successful brands tell a story that resonates with their customer base to the extent that customers integrate these brands into their own life stories.

In this context, "*Brand Storytelling in the Digital Age: Theories, Practice and Application*" makes a contribution drawing on insights from interdisciplinary literature on storytelling with a particular focus on brand storytelling and narrative theories.

Chapter 1 sets the context by substantiating the influential role of storytelling linked to our evolution and how it has shifted the mindset of brand marketers. Then, Chapter 2 provides a critical review of the interdisciplinary theories of storytelling covering the domains of narrative theories, consumer psychology, research in branding and tourism. Here—drawing on seminal research—the author critically synthesises the interdisciplinary literature and tells a compelling story of how control of marketing is shifting from marketers to consumers in the digital age, coupled with the power of social media-driven connectivity.

Chapter 3 covers the science of storytelling drawing on neuroscience's research that intersects with consumer behaviour and branding. With theories and case studies, this chapter presents how stories make changes in the consumers' brains and drive emotion, trust and cooperation—to which marketers need to pay attention. With several case studies and examples, Chapter 4 explains different types of brand stories, which are rooted in the literature on emotion, persuasion, and the constructivist brand paradigm. This chapter highlights the art of brand storytelling and best practices.

Chapter 5 critically covers the essential elements of a story drawing upon interdisciplinary narrative theories covering narrative structure, characterisation, plots, Hero's Journey framework, heroic transformation and story themes. This chapter makes a fascinating contribution to the application of brand storytelling with a conceptual framework which practitioners will find helpful. Finally, Chapter 6 shows the author's position on the future of storytelling shaped by AI, VI, AR and big data. This chapter also plays an essential part in shaping the new research and industry practices in the post-modern era.

The book is a fantastic achievement and brings together some fascinating research from a broad range of disciplines. It should be of interest to managers and academics alike.

Professor Heidi Winklhofer
Professor of Marketing and Associate Editor for the Journal of Services Marketing
Head of the Marketing Division, Nottingham University Business School
University of Nottingham—Jubilee Campus
Nottingham, UK

Preface

We are living in the most advanced time in the history of the world where science has transformed all aspects of our lives. We can connect with almost anyone in any corner of the world in seconds by the touch of a phone screen. Information is just a search engine click away. Science, technology, creativity, innovation, art and commerce are at, perhaps, a new pinnacle, bringing the world to our fingertips. Curiosity, creativity, and innovation have empowered humankind to achieve things that were once unthinkable. It is not only the power of our imagination but also the ancient art of storytelling that has impacted our world, our lives. The advancement of neuroscience reveals that storytelling has the power to release certain hormones in our brains, which increases our disposition to trust and foster our collective co-operation, turning our ideas into reality.

Storytelling moves our hearts, allowing us to connect with each other through emotional glue: empowering us with hopes and aspirations; transforming our imagination into dreams; our dreams into visions; and our visions into missions. When we tell relatable stories, others can believe what we believe; they can see too what we can see. This is not stories of magic rather the magic of stories that make us human when we tell them to others in the right way. Every brand tells stories, but only a few brands tell them in the right way.

Storytelling has always been an inseparable part of humankind. It has been the critical element of the marketer's toolkit and the language of brand communication, travelling from the age of cave art to the age of the computer screen. However, in the age of social media-driven connectedness and the post-advertising era, the art of brand storytelling is transforming, and it is changing fast.

This book reveals how storytelling has evolved from ancient art to a contemporary marketing science in the age of continued digital transformation. Through critical analyses of the existing theories, practices and applications of storytelling, it provides a platform for academics, researchers and practitioners to converse, enabling them to use the interdisciplinary lens to engage with the research in the fields of neuroscience, emotional attachment, and narrative theories.

The dramatic shift in brand storytelling has seen marketers in the driving seat while consumers are navigating. With the increased speed of technological advancements and the development of new media platforms, we will potentially witness a revolutionary shift in the way brands connect with their customers through unforgettable stories, created at the intersection of science, art, and humanity. Being creative, bringing novelty and transparency, empathising with the customers, keeping them at the centre, treating them as heroes while brands playing the role of mentors, and nurturing the human spirit are going to be the fundamental driving forces for the brands to flourish.

London, UK
July 2020

S M A Moin

Acknowledgements

First of all, my sincere gratitude to my Creator, who has given me life and created me as a human being, the storytelling animal.

Then my heartfelt thanks to my wife and two sons for their heart-melting love, generous support, and exceptional patience while I was busy writing this book.

I am also indebted to my elder brother, M A Zaman, without whose unconditional love, support, and guidance, I could never find my passion for storytelling and pursue my dream to spread my thoughts.

My special thanks to my mentor, Jonathan Groucutt, for sharing his invaluable knowledge from time to time when I needed it, which has helped me to reflect critically; seeing the world through a set of different lenses.

I would also like to thank my fellow academic colleagues at Coventry University London, for their encouragement and interest in my research. Finally, I would like to thank my students over the years who have provided lively debate and enriching discussions on this important topic.

Praise for *Brand Storytelling in the Digital Age*

"Brand narratives in the age of social media and digital transformation are essential to the survival of contemporary brands. This book adopts an interdisciplinary approach drawing on the author's expertise in neuroscience, consumer behavior, and branding taking the readers on an avid scientific journey around the brand narrative and storytelling discourse. The book presents an excellent entry point for scholars and Ph.D. researchers interested in advancing the growing field of brand storytelling especially in the digital age."

—Noha El-Bassiouny, *Vice Dean for Academic Affairs, The German University in Cairo, Egypt*

"More and more companies and brands are engaging in storytelling in the form of content marketing. As social media has accelerated growth in this practice, it is important that academics fully understand the theories, practices and applications of storytelling. This book is a welcome addition to the literature as it provides a valuable overview of current thinking in this area supported by examples and case studies."

—Alan Wilson, *Professor of Marketing, University of Strathclyde Business School*

"The smart money is on learning how brands can make waves in an age where smart minds, smart mouths, and smart thumbs are congregating around smart phones and surfing more content than ever before. This book provides valuable insight, from a number of perspectives, into how brands can build momentum through the art of storytelling."

—Jonathan A.J. Wilson, *Professor of Brand Strategy & Culture, Regent's University London*

"In this timely book, Moin takes the reader on an exploratory journey of storytelling. By adopting the interdisciplinary approach and drawing on theory and practice, the author encourages marketing academics and practitioners to pause and reflect on how consumers really think when choosing a brand."

—Hanna Yakavenka, *Associate Dean of Internationalisation and Business Development, Coventry University London*

"If you are a Ph.D. student and storytelling is your research methodology, then this book is a must read. This book does a good job of explaining how the history of storytelling is linked to human evolution and in doing this, each chapters navigates through different views and perspective, including marketing and branding strategy."

—Hany Wells, *Associate Dean of Student Experience and Quality Assurance, Coventry University London*

"Facts are forgotten; stories stick. This truth is revealed in creative and memorable stories that survive in the digital deluge. Strong narratives bring brands to life, then brands become part of the storyline in a consumer's own life. This is the powerful potential of digital marketing, as Moin explains."

—J Graham Spickett-Jones, *Head of Department for Marketing, Fashion, Hospitality and Tourism, Coventry University London*

"Moin's new book provides a fresh perspective on storytelling through interdisciplinary study. This book poses questions and encourages reflexivity of brand storytelling in today's fast-paced and digitally driven society. It is a welcome addition to brand management and would certainly inspire further interests and research by readers."

—Gordon Yan, *Principal Lecturer in Hospitality and Tourism, Coventry University London*

"Whether you are a Marketing Director, Cloud Service Project Manager or Sales Executive, you have to communicate with people. In this book. Moin shows how storytelling is disrupting the brand communications in the age of digital transformation. It is a guide for the Digital Marketers and for all who want to know how customers think."

—Enamul Haque, *Associate Director, Cloud Infrastructure Services*

"Storytelling is the currency of marketing. In this book, with an interdisciplinary approach, Moin has unveiled the magic codes of storytelling that, while serving the researchers, will also equip the practitioners to connect with their customers emotionally. The book draws insights from the sound theories of neuroscience, emotion, and brand narrative, providing cutting-edge knowledge on brand storytelling. Brand marketers will find it as their guidebook of storytelling."

—Ben Botes, *General Partner, SLC Impact Investment*

"A fantastic book for researchers and practitioners who want to learn about the use of the ancient art of storytelling in modern-day contexts. It blends theories, practices and applications by drawing on a range of disciplines; making it a credible and enjoyable source for storytelling enthusiasts."

—Sabrina Vieth, *Principal Lecturer in Entrepreneurship and Innovation, Coventry University London*

"This book has everything about the Art and Science of Brand Storytelling. This is a guide for every brand and corporate manager who wants to connect with their customers using the power of storytelling."

—Hafiz A. Mujahid, *Head of Human Resources, UN World Food Programme*

"Engineers too need to understand how people think so that they can develop products that speak to the customers. This book explains storytelling from the perspective of neuroscience and gives a platform for marketers and non-marketers to converse while designing happiness for their customers."

—Mohammad Shahin Ahsan, *Principal Engineer, Broadcom Inc.*

"Seen through the lens of neuroscience, emotion and cognition, Moin, in this book, deconstructs the codes of Brand Storytelling for researchers and more importantly for marketing practitioners."

—Joe Shami, *Management Consultant, London*

"This book combines the art of storytelling in light of theory and practices with the nature and sciences of mind, heart and brain to unleash the power of storified narratives for branding and marketing of any products or services. If consultants combine their deep critical thinking, problem solving and analytical skills with the tools of story-telling they can communicate the findings of any project at hand in a manner that is really powerful and persuasive to the stakeholder clients."

—Sabbir Ahmed, *Consultant, Aerospace & Defence*

"Moin provides a thoughtful toolkit for branding and marketing communication researchers and practitioners on how to develop sustainable consumer centric relationships through the art and science of storytelling. In a world of information overload, fake news and rising consumer backlash, this book provides a much needed contribution to having authentic and honest narratives."

—Ranjit Thind, *Author,* Strategic Fashion Management: Concepts, Model and Strategies for Competitive Advantage

"Moin uses the magical language of storytelling, to ignite readers' true passion for solving the puzzle of brand communication in the era of digitisation by connecting ancient art, neuroscience, theories, and many more fascinating pieces."

—Lin Su, *Senior Lecturer in Marketing, Coventry University London*

"Storytelling is the most potent communication tactic in the time when people are easily distracted due to information-overload. With an interdisciplinary approach, in this book, Moin synthesised the theories, practices and applications of brand storytelling drawing on narrative theories. This book will not only benefit the brand practitioners and researchers but also help the educators to harness the emotional and magical power of storytelling in connecting with digital learners."

—Orhan Demirovski, *Education Consultant, Experientia Ltd.*

Contents

List of Figures

List of Tables

CHAPTER 1

Introduction: The Ancient Art of Storytelling and the Language of Marketing

Abstract Storytelling inextricably links to our human evolution, providing us with the means to survive against the odds. For its astonishing power to communicate and connect wrapped with emotion, storytelling has evolved from ancient art to contemporary marketing science. This chapter sets the context by highlighting the power of storytelling as a language of marketing and brand communication, touching and influencing all aspects of our lives. As natural storytellers, human beings behave like storytelling animals. It has ingrained in our psyche, with researchers arguing that it is not something that we as human beings do but something that defines us. The opening chapter provides a roadmap to navigate through the rest of the chapters, inviting you to join the debate on the role of brand storytelling in the digital age.

Keywords Ancient art, positivistic-brand paradigm · Interpretive-brand paradigm · Brand-centric mindset · Customer-centric mindset · Brand storytelling myths, mystery and maxim

Storytelling is an ancient art that played a crucial role in our evolution as a social animal who can neither stop talking nor stop bonding. Today, through a series of transformation, it has become a language that dominates marketing and brand communications in the contemporary world. Not just in the modern-day, it has dominated the marketing of all

S M A Moin, *Brand Storytelling in the Digital Age*,
https://doi.org/10.1007/978-3-030-59085-7_1

ages. Nevertheless, in the contemporary world, the power of connectivity (Krevolin 2016) coming from the advancement in the digital and mobile technology coupled with the proliferation of social media in all aspects of our lives has revolutionised the way brands tell stories (Henning-Thurau et al. 2013). Storytelling is not just a crucial part of marketing; it is an essential part of our lives (Van Laer et al. 2014). It has embedded in our DNA (McKee and Gerace 2018).

Since time immemorial, storytelling has been an intricate part of our lives. Human beings are known as "homo narrans" (Lund et al. 2018), meaning "storytelling human" or natural storytellers (Niles 1999). It helped the human race to survive in the test of time. At night, ancient people used to gather around the fire to share their adventure of hunting and the tactics they employed for their survival from the wild attacks through the art of storytelling. Storytelling has connected human beings, fostering cooperation through sharing their feelings and emotions—leading to the formation of tribes, communities, nations, and a global village. Storytelling has not only sharpened their skills for their survival but also helped them evolve from "Homo sapiens" (Harari 2014) to Homo Deus (Harari 2016) who mastered the power over other species. Irrespective of their colour, ethnicity, nationality, religion, and different backgrounds, people exposed themselves to stories (Van Laer et al. 2014) since childhood, living with them until the last day of their lives; and when they die what remains is nothing but stories.

> … parents tell their children bedtime stories about dragons and castles, teachers tell their students stories about history and society, musicians sing their fans stories about budding and fading romances, organisations tell their stakeholders stories about their past performances and future goals, and novelists tell their readers stories about possible lives in possible worlds. (Sanders and Krieken 2018, p. 1)

Ancient Art in the Contemporary World

Storytelling has become part of our social fabric, travelling through the ages—from the age of cave art to the age of computer screen (Nanton and Dicks 2013)—as a powerful means of communication and bonding. Multiple research across disciplines support that stories have the power to attract attention as well as engage with people both intellectually and emotionally (McKee and Gerace 2018; Wachtman and Johnson 2009).

For its astonishing power of connecting with the consumers (Garmston 2019; Chiu et al. 2012), storytelling has evolved from ancient art to contemporary marketing science. To connect with the consumers and to influence the prospects, brand marketers and advertising professionals use storytelling as an effective tool (Rose 2011) to break the clutter and noise and get attention through attaching meaning to brands. Thus, storytelling is so prevalent in the digital age when people are bombarded with loads of messages, and noise is the norm. Brand stories save the brands in the hearts of their customers who find meaning through brand experience, brand engagement and brand consumption.

Evolution of Branding

Before discussing brand storytelling in detail, it is logical to give a brief account of the evolution of branding to have an understanding of its relevance in brand communication. The concept of branding has changed significantly with time. During their evolution in all aspects of our lives, brands have embraced different forms of storytelling. Gabay (2015) finds that one of the very earlier notion of brand originates from the pursuit of power and pleasure by the symbol of an eagle used by Julius Caesar. After that, the concept of brand has gone through several stages (Gabay 2015):

- Ownership
- Identification
- Features
- Benefits
- Experience
- Identity
- Inclusion

The concept of ownership was popular in the 1800s. At that time, the brands were proofs of ownership of goods: to whom they belong and who made them. After the invention of railways, as the long-distance distribution of goods started in the 1890s, brands became symbols of identifying the manufacturers. In the 1900s, brands started to signify the functional attributes of the products by focusing on the most distinct and differentiating features. In the 1930s, the focus of branding shifted from tangible features to intangible benefits.

In the 1960s, the focus of brand included experience, which eventually extended to service branding. In the 2000s, brands focused on identity. People started to find meaning in brands to express themselves to others. As stories attach meaning to brands, throughout the process of evolution, brands told different stories to create desired meaning. Table 1.1 briefly shows how the concept and focus of branding has shifted over time.

The old school of branding was more interested in using the concept of the brand as a means to identify and differentiate the products of one manufacturer from the others by using the name, term, sign, symbol, and design. However, the contemporary thinking of branding treats brand as a multidimensional construct, which calls for a comprehensive understanding and requires multidimensional thinking and multidisciplinary perspectives including economics, strategic management, organisational behaviour, consumer research, psychology, and anthropology (Heding et al. 2009). Drawing upon from a multidisciplinary approach, they have identified two brand management paradigms: positivistic and constructivist.

Table 1.1 How the concept and focus of branding has shifted over time

Timeline	*Concept of brand*	*Meaning*
1800s	Ownership and identification	To whom brands belong to
1890s		Identifying the manufacturers of the products
1900s	Feature	*What it has*: product specification or functional attributes of the products (brand stands as a guarantor of quality)
1930s	Benefits	*What it does*: mostly include the emotional and intangible benefits of the products (brand stands as a guarantor of quality)
1960s	Experience	*How it feels*: the feeling of customer for owning the brands
2000s	Identity	*Who you are*: how the use of brand shapes consumer's identity
Now	Brand inclusion	What people share

Source Adapted from Gabay (2015, pp. 15–16)

Positivistic Brand Management Paradigm

The positivistic brand paradigm promotes the idea that marketers (active end) own the brands and control the brand communication, whereas consumers simply receive the communication (passive end). In this paradigm, brand equity is created by marketers and brand is perceived as "a manipulable lifeless artefact (products plus that is created by its owner/ managers and that can be positioned, segmented, and used to create an image)" (Hanby 1999, p. 12).

Constructivist Brand Management Paradigm

In constructivist—often also known as interpretive—paradigm, both marketers and the consumers co-create the brands. Here, both marketers and consumers actively interact with each other in the creation of brand values and brand meaning. According to Hanby (1999), brands are perceived more like living entities with the ability to form relationships that evolve and changes over time:

- "As holistic entities with many characteristics of living beings" (p. 10).
- "As a living entity (with a personality with which we can form a relationship and that can exchange and evolve over time)" (p. 12).

Triggered by interdisciplinary research, the shift from "positivist paradigm" to "constructivist paradigm" happened incrementally throughout 1990 with the relational approach to branding played a vital role (Heding et al. 2009). Thus, over the past two decades, the definition and concept of the brand have transformed significantly.

A Significant Shift in the Definition of Brand

In 1960, American Marketing Association defined "brand" as "name, term, sign, symbol, design, or a combination of them, intended to identify the goods or services of one seller or group of sellers and to differentiate them from those of competitors." Thirty-eight year later, in 1998, Chernatony and Riley (1998) defined "brand" as "a complex multidimensional construct whereby managers augment products and services with values and this facilitates the process by which consumer confidently recognise and appreciate these values" (p. 436).

Consequently, a number of brand constructs such as brand attitude, brand affect, brand attachment, brand love, brand personality, brand identity, brand image, brand experience, and brand meaning have emerged with their measurement scales to conceptualise brand in a sophisticated way. As branding becomes an integral part of our social fabric due to our engagement and experience with brands and given that human beings are storytelling animals (Gottschall 2012), marketers found storytelling as the more effective and humanistic approach not only to design brand communication but also managing brand strategy as a whole (Delgado-Ballester and Fernández-Sabiote 2016). Thus, in the contemporary world, we cannot imagine branding without brand storytelling. It is the story that attaches meaning to brands so that customers can relate with the brands.

Evolution of Brand Storytelling and the Post-advertising Era

Although storytelling is now a critical element of the overall brand strategy, it entered into marketing through advertising (McKee and Gerace 2018). Since the 1700s, when Benjamin Franklin launched the "Pennsylvania Gazette", consumers have seen various forms of advertising that used stories as carriers to communicate the brand and product messages to the target customers. The advancement in technologies and the proliferation of multiple media in our lives, marketers have adopted different tactics while advertising: eventually we have seen the rise and fall of advertising, bring us in the post-advertising era (McKee and Gerace 2018; Jiwa 2014). The evolution of advertising and the shift of brand storytelling can be categorised into three major waves.

First Wave: Story-Addictive Interruption

The first wave of storytelling can be termed as story-addictive interruption, commencing around the time of the inception of the weekly newspaper in the 1700s. This was mainly a subscription-based model of publication, which focussed on disseminating stories about everyday life (including products) and politics (McKee and Gerace 2018). However, the combination of a low subscription and circulation base could not sustain this form of media for very long. This, in turn, forced the evolution of a new business model: the development of print advertising. As money started pouring in, the newspaper publishers invented numerous incentives to attract businesses to advertise. These advertisements began to create a brand awareness, which the companies found as an effective way to enhance customer acquisition and retention. Thus through the incorporation of adverting publishers found a sustainable business model.

The development of radio and commercial television services, in addition to a burgeoning print media, provided the space for advertisers to market an increasing range of products and services; most especially from the 1950s onwards. The development of the Internet, the opening up—though deregulation—of media outlets and the introduction of new digital technologies provided a diverse range of platforms that created a new media landscape. This landscape fuelled the growth in advertising yet also created various shifts in emphasis including a move from a print-base to an online one. Moreover, the digital revolution also allowed consumer to be more "active" in how they responded to, for example, TV commercials. Technology now provided consumers to "fast forward" or to even skip advertisements altogether. Thus the bypassing of advertising, in addition to potentially affecting brand revenues, has also encouraged marketers to seek new and enhanced ways of communicating their messages to the current and new customers. This includes finding new ways of brand storytelling.

Second Wave: Deceptive-Story Manipulation

Over the period, marketers have not just reached to their customers using the interruption model, they have also used the taproot marketing logic through two forms of communications: rational and emotional (McKee and Gerace 2018) drawing on critical marketing theories. This marks the beginning of the second wave, the deceptive-story manipulation, considering humankind as rational beings who selects brands through a decision-making process using facts and figures against a set of criteria. In their book, STORYNOMICS: Story-Driven Marketing in the Post-Adverting World, McKee and Gerace (2018) have given an elaborative explanation of how some advertisements have used rational and emotional marketing to deceive the customers. However, not all marketing initiatives are deceiving. There are many countries, for instance, the UK and Europe, where strict regulations prohibit deceptive marketing that exploits customers and reduces competition. Nonetheless, rational approaches to marketing have encouraged marketers to exploit rhetorical marketing. In these cases, a brand uses a set of criteria that bring its products the top. What they do is carefully omit the criteria where competitors' products outperform.

However, this tactic has not been effective in the long run: "In a world of immediate, global information flow, exaggerated, underperforming claims backfire. Consumers compare marketing promises with their real-world experience, and when two don't line up, they mock the brands that played them with scathing product reviews, public tweets, and Facebook posts. Through decades of false promises, marketers have trained the consumers to distrust advertising" (McKee and Gerace 2018, pp. 19–20).

Although emotion is a powerful glue to connect with the customers (Krevolin 2016), some advertisers have used emotion as a way of manipulating customers (McKee and Gerace 2018) by using two primary types of emotion: pleasure and pain (Damasio 2005). Bloom (2011) explained that pleasure and pain are not just sensory stimuli but also depend on our belief and perceptions. The existing research supports this proposition by revealing the relationship between high price and perception of higher (or) quality (or taste). McKee and Gerace (2018) further argue that manipulation through emotion uses two techniques: seduction with a promise of pleasure and coercion with a threat of pain. Due to significant gap between the promised and actual experience with the brand, the savvy customers who come across thousands of advertisements every day are no more driven by emotional manipulation which is why about 66% of millennials prefer to pay to block ads (McKee and Gerace 2018). The marketing initiative focusing only on sales by any means trains customers not only to resist but also revolt, leaving with only one option: storytelling (McKee and Gerace 2018), which is linked with our evolution and which makes us human (Gottschall 2012). Within authentic storytelling (the third wave), transparency is the key, which not only focuses on communication but also on connection.

Third Wave: Authentic Story-Driven Connection

We are living in the age of connectivity driven by the permeating and relatively inexpensive and proliferated wireless broadband, fastest-growing mobile technology, and social media mediated peer-to-peer communication. As a result, marketing is changing with the power of authentic, relevant, and experiential storytelling. Social media is shifting the power from marketers to consumers where the story told by the consumers themselves are often more potent than the ones told by the brands (Walter and Gioglio 2019). Authentic storytelling does not exploit rational and emotional communication as a means of manipulation; instead, it uses the power of storytelling honestly and sincerely to connect with the customer at a deeper level. Authentic storytelling invites customers on a transformational journey through a rational message wrapped in emotion.

"A well-told story captures our attention, holds us in suspense, and pays off with a meaningful emotional experience" (McKee and Gerace 2018, p. 29).

A well-told brand story use characters through whose eyes the customer can see the world and be empathetic for the character. Customers therefore can relate to the character. Through demonstrating the day-to-day life challenges of their customers, strong brands hold their hands as a mentor rather than the hero (Donald 2017).

The Myths, Mystery, and Maxim of Brand Storytelling

Although storytelling is with us since time immemorial and used by the brands in different forms and formats, there are many myths about storytelling. There are differences in opinion—coined as war—between the left-brain executives who focus on reality and the right-brain marketers who focus on perception (Ries and Ries 2009). Besides, not all brands know how to tell the right story, at the right time, in the right way (Walter and Gioglio 2019). Many brands spend a considerable budget towards marketing, but the story they tell through advertising and other means of communication do not stick with their customers. There are several myths and mysteries of storytelling, which are influencing marketers' perception of storytelling.

Storytelling Is for Entertainment, Not Branding

The left-brain executives often argue that storytelling is for entertainment that is suitable for attracting children. They often believe storytelling is not suitable for a critical management activity linking to several performance indicators: profit margin, shareholders value, and productivity.

However, Senik (2009) argues that critical business activity involved understanding people psychology to deal with all the stakeholders, including employees, clients, suppliers, customers, and fans. Successful storytelling companies need to shift their mindset towards a more transparent, authentic and humanistic business model centred on people. Authenticity is at the heart of branding (Aaker 2018) and the authentic and trustworthy companies do not claim things that they do not stand for. The maxim of storytelling is that it is with us since time immemorial and part of our evolution as the most influential species in the world. Thus, authentic brand stories are critical for brand positioning and attracting the attention of the right set of customers.

Brand Storytelling Equals Adverts Plus Stories

There is a myth that storytelling is a way of communicating through stories, which leads to an understanding that commercials with stories destine to succeed. There is a mystery that storytelling is not merely a technique of copy and paste, a checklist to follow, and a guideline to adhere. Indeed, storytelling is much more than a checklist or a set of rules. However, the maxim of brand storytelling suggests that it is a sophisticated art where rules guide but do not make the process mechanistic. McKee and Gerace (2018) compared storytelling with art and music, which demands a quest to muster the skill: “Many assumes that because they’ve seen and heard a lifetime of stories, they could easily create one. But that’s like thinking you can compose music because you’ve been to concerts” (p. 29).

Brand Storytelling Is a Tactic, Not a Philosophy

Another myth and mystery of brand storytelling suggest that it is tactic to deliver a marketing message. Often viewed as a trend, companies do it as everyone does it. Often it is viewed as a way of staying relevant. This understanding often leads the brands to develop stories that lack authenticity or perceived as fake. In the absence of authenticity and transparency, the brand stories fail to resonate with the customers. The maxim of brand storytelling is that it has a root far deeper than tactics. Brand storytelling has crossed the arena of advertising and playing a crucial role in delivering the overall brand strategy, which stems from brand philosophy. Brand storytelling as a philosophy approaches to understanding the culture of the organisation - how it treats employees, customers, and stakeholder. The brand philosophy also depicts the founder's passion, brand's purpose, its attitude towards humanity, and how it manifest authenticity and benevolence. In other words, the clarity of the core brand values by every brand stakeholders shape the culture where authentic stories emerge. The culture and philosophy of the organisation shape the brand philosophy and the brand philosophy shape the art of brand storytelling.

Brand Storytelling in the Digital Age

Brand storytelling should not be viewed as a marketing strategy to manipulate consumers' perceptions with a well-articulated brand message wrapped with narratives that are not authentic. Instead, it is the way brands create an unforgettable customer experience through all customer touchpoints by actually doing things that touch customers' hearts. Thus, when an authentic brand story is told customers have no reason not to believe and engage with. It is not about developing a brand slogan by employing consultants who do not experience real business as employees or customers do. Instead, real brand storytelling emerges through developing an organic culture by manifesting the brand philosophy consistently to bring brand values to life. It is about empowering the customers with the experience that they cannot help not sharing with their connections.

"It is an impression you create at every single touchpoint of the customer experience journey. From packaging to customer care, everything you do – and how you do it – becomes a story. It becomes your brand. It's not just about the stories you tell; it's also about the stories your customers create after they engage with you" (Walter and Gioglio 2019, p. 258).

Brand storytelling is most potent when stories are authentic, transparent, and emerge naturally that customers do not even recognise those as marketing activities (Walter and Gioglio 2019). Thus, most of the time, the best brand stories tend to be customers' stories, developed when they have an extraordinary experience with the brands. Moreover, customers cannot stop sharing these experiences with others in the form of stories.

In the digital age of connectivity driven by social media, these kinds of stories not only create brand tribes but also empower the consumers to be the active brand storytellers. The brands that win the hearts and minds nurture customers' dreams and desires, care for them, and connect with them at a deeper level through fostering authenticity and passion. The result is phenomenal: prospects know the brand and become leads, leads like the brand and become customers (Dib 2018), customers trust the brands and become advocates, advocates believe what the brands believe and become a brand tribe. The digital canvas offered by social media enables the brand to be purposeful and manifest the brand values through involving customers.

Where Art Meets with Science and Technology

The digital age brings both opportunities and challenges for the marketers. The social media landscape in the digital era increases the degree of communications between brands and customers, and customers and customers through the emergence of multiple channels. Customers now can connect with almost anyone in any corner of the world in seconds by the touch of a phone screen. Information is just a search engine click away. The technology has given customers the power to further promote a brand message or respond negatively when they feel manipulated through online conversations with others. The control over the brand message is shifting from marketers to customers, who now have the tools to create stories and messages that may either enhance the brand reputation or destroy it. The winning brands are the ones who provide seamless brand experience and create story worlds where multiple co-creators develop stories in the digital space that shows brand consumer-brand bonding and engagement. The new tools and technologies and the free digital space have empowered the customers to be artists, developing creative and telling brand stories that are more effective and believable. Brand marketers are becoming more like directors and screenwriters who create a digital space and write the act, inviting customers on a hero's journey to find their identity, pursue their dream and unleash their best with the help of the brand. When customers values align with the brand values, and customers and brands create a shared experience that is worth spreading into the digitally connected world, an art emerges in the form of brand story that is far more powerful than traditional ad and resonate with the customers.

The Roadmap

The rest of the chapters provide a roadmap of this book through introducing several significant strands of storytelling that originate from different disciplines but form as an essential basis for the storytelling in marketing with a focus on brand storytelling. The Roadmap of the "Brand Storytelling in the Digital Age: Theories, Practice and Application" (Fig. 1.1) will help the reader to navigate through different topics covered in this manuscript, helping them join the debate of storytelling in the digital age.

At the heart of brand storytelling, are the customers and not the brands—particularly more relevant in the digital age, where the consumers have conquered the social media landscape. Successful brands understand their customers' pain points better and know exactly where their customers are currently. The brands that connect with their customers at a deeper level do not speak louder about their products and services. Instead, they know how to:

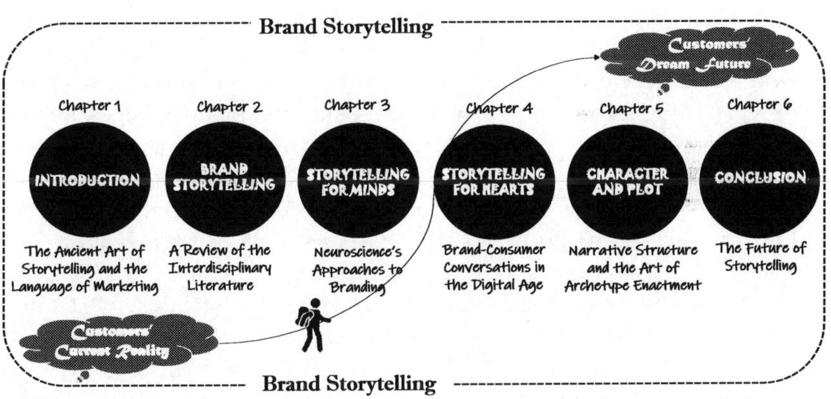

Fig. 1.1 A roadmap of "Brand Storytelling in the Digital Age: Theories, Practice and Application" (*Source* Developed by author)

- Craft and tell compelling brand stories that resonate with their customers emotionally,
- Provide their customers meaning, which unites them as a brand tribe and find their identity,
- Treat their customers as heroes and show a clear path to navigate towards their dream future.

The book has encapsulated this secret art of brand storytelling in six chapters linking the theories, practice, and applications.

Introduction: The Ancient Art of Storytelling and the Language of Marketing (Chapter 1) sets the context by providing a rationale for brand storytelling in the digital age of connectivity mediated by the innovation and advancement in the mobile technologies and social media being part of our social fabric. This chapter unveils the incredible power of brand storytelling in communicating the brand values and creating an emotional bond between the brands and the customers.

Brand Storytelling: A Review of the Interdisciplinary Literature (Chapter 2) gives a critical review of the interdisciplinary theories of storytelling. This chapter will explain several theories, principles and critical elements of storytelling grounded from the existing storytelling literature drawing on different disciplines. Thus, this chapter provides an in-depth theoretical understanding to the researchers and practitioners, helping them to manifest sound principles while creating and communicating brand stories.

Storytelling is not a science; it is an art—an ancient art connected to human civilisation. However, there is profound science behind it—this science can explain the incredible power of storytelling: why it works. Storytelling for Minds: Neuroscience's Approaches to Branding (Chapter 3) explains how stories influence consumer psychology and behaviour drawing on insights from research in neuroscience and how brand marketers tap into this invaluable research findings. The chapter explains that biological changes in the brain triggered by stories can influence consumer psychology and create emotional bonding between storytellers and story listeners.

Storytelling for Hearts: Brand-Consumer Conversations in the Digital Age (Chapter 4) explains the various types of brand stories and their incredible power in connecting with the consumers. This chapter also exemplifies the manifestation of storytelling principles through critically analysing several strategic and tactical brand stories that have fostered consumer engagement in the digital landscape. While Chapter 3 focuses on the science of storytelling, Chapter 4 focus on the art of manifesting this science.

Character and Plot: Narrative Structure and the Art of Archetype Enactment (Chapter 5) gives a critical review of the narrative theories, narrative structure, and the art of creating and enacting characters in the context of brand stories. This chapter will also introduce a model incorporating the essential elements and principles of storytelling that helps the researchers deconstruct brand stories to make sense of the gap between the theories and practice. This will also help the practitioners with a framework to think, plan and create brand stories.

Conclusion: The Future of Storytelling (Chapter 6) briefly summarises the essential insights of the previous chapters with particular focus on the shift in brand storytelling in the digital age. The chapter also brings some discussions, predicting the future of storytelling in the rapidly changing digital age, which is somehow unclear and mysterious. This will be interesting and useful for helping researchers with the direction of future research on brand storytelling.

References

Aaker, D. (2018). *Creating Signature Stories: Strategic Messaging That Energies, Persuades and Inspire*. New York: Morgan James Publishing.

Bloom, P. (2011). *How Pleasure Works: Why We Like What We Like*. London: Vintage.

Chernatony, L., & Riley, F. D. (1998). Defining a 'Brand': Beyond the Literature with Experts' Interpretations. *Journal of Marketing Management, 14*(5), 417–443.

Chiu, H. C., Hsieh, Y. C., & Kuo, Y. C. (2012). How to Align Your Brand Stories with Your Products. *Journal of Retailing, 88*(2), 262–275.

Damasio, A. R. (2005). *DESCARTES ERROR: Emotion, Reason and the Human Brain*. London: Vintage.

Delgado-Ballester, E., & Fernández-Sabiote, E. (2016). "Once Upon a Brand": Storytelling Practices by Spanish Brands. *Spanish Journal of Marketing, 20*(2), 115–131.

Dib, A. (2018). *The 1-Page Marketing Plan: Get Customers, Make More Money, and Stand Out from the Crowd*. Miami: Successwise.

Donald, M. (2017). *Building a Story Brand: Clarify Your Message so Customers Will Listen*. Nashville: HarperCollins Leadership.

Gabay, J. (2015). *Brand Psychology: Consumer Perceptions, Corporate Reputations*. London: Kogan Page Limited.

Garmston, R. J. (2019). *The Astonishing Power of Storytelling: Leading, Teaching and Transforming in a New Way*. Thousand Oaks, CA: Corwin.

Gottschall, J. (2012). *The Storytelling Animal: How Stories Make Us Human*. New York: Mariner.

Hanby, T. (1999). Brands Dead or Alive. *Journal of Market Research Society, 41*(1), 9–19.

Harari, Y. N. (2014). *Sapiens: A Brief History of Humankind*. London: Harvill Sacker.

Harari, Y. N. (2016). *Homo Deus: A Brief History of Tomorrow*. London: Vintage Publishing.

Heding, T., Knudtzen, C., & Bjerre, M. (2009). *Brand Management: Research, Theory, and Practice*. Abingdon, Oxon: Routledge.

Henning-Thurau, H., Hofacker, C. F., & Bloching, B. (2013). Marketing the Pinball Way: Understanding How Social Media Change the Generation of Value for Consumers and Companies. *Journal of Interactive Marketing, 2*, 237–241.

Jiwa, B. (2014). *Difference: The One-Page Method for Reimaging Your Business and Reinventing Your Marketing*. Australia: The Story of Telling Press. https://www.amazon.co.uk/Difference-one-page-reimagining-reinventing-marketing/dp/1494842718/ref=sr_1_1?dchild=1&keywords=difference%2C+JIWA&qid=1602355179&s=books&sr=1-1.

Krevolin, R. (2016). *The Hook: How to Share Your Brand's Unique Story to Engage Customers, Boost Sales, and Achieve Heartfelt Success*. Wayne: The Career Press Inc.

Lund, N. F., Cohen, S. A., & Scarles, C. (2018, June). The Power of Social Media Storytelling in Destination Branding. *Journal of Destination Marketing & Management, 8*, 271–280.

McKee, R., & Gerace, T. (2018). *Storynomics: Story-Driven Marketing in the Post-Advertising World*. York: Methuen.

Nanton, N., & Dicks, J. (2013). *Story Selling: Hollywood Secret Revealed How to Sell Without Selling*. Winter Park, FL: Celebrity Press.

Niles, J. D. (1999). *Homo Narran: The Poetics and Anthropology of Oral Literature*. Philadelphia: University of Pennsylvania Press.

Ries, A., & Ries, L. (2009). *War in the Boardroom: Why Left-Brain Management and Right-Brain Marketing Don't See Eye-to-Eye—And What to Do About It*. New York: HarpersCollins.

Rose, F. (2011). The Art of Immersion: How the Digital Generation Is Remaking Hollywood, Madison Avenue, and the Way We Tell Stories. *International Journal of Advertising, 30*(5), 915–919.

Sanders, J., & van Krieken, K. (2018). Exploring Narrative Structure and Hero Enactment in Brand Stories. *Frontiers in Psychology*, *9*, 1–17.

Senik, S. (2009). *Start with Why: How Great Leaders Inspire Everyone to Take Action*. London: Penguin.

Van Laer, T., Ruyter, K. D., Vsconti, L. M., & Wetzels, M. (2014). The Extended Transportation-Imagery Model: A Meta-Analysis of the Antecedents and Consequences of Consumers' Narrative Transportation. *Journal of Consumer Research*, *40*(5), 797–817.

Wachtman, E., & Johnson, L. S. (2009). The Persuasive Power of Story. *Marketing Management*, *18*(1), 28–34.

Walter, E., & Gioglio, J. (2019). *The Laws of Brand Storytelling: Win—And Keep—Your Customers' Hearts and Mind*. New York: McGraw-Hill.

CHAPTER 2

Brand Storytelling: A Review of the Interdisciplinary Literature

Abstract The power of digital technologies and social media has transformed the way brands talk to their customers. Contemporary marketing is less about the products we make and the services we offer, but more about the experiences brands create, giving customers numerous stories to tell. This chapter presents a critical review of the interdisciplinary theories of storytelling drawing on narrative philosophy, consumer psychology, research in branding and tourism. While covering the essential elements of a story, it also highlights the shift from predictable bowling to pinball wizardry due to the rapid advancement of digital technology and proliferation of social media in all aspects of our lives. The chapter also draws on the neuroscience's perspective of how the brain responses to storytelling and reviews different approaches to brand research with associated brand storytelling.

Keywords Interdisciplinary research · Essential story elements · Narrative transportation · Experiential outcome · Moral sense making · Brain's response to storytelling

Storytelling, known as an ancient art (Gallo 2016; Krevolin 2016), is a powerful social phenomenon and one of the oldest forms of communication (Kaufman 2003; Worth 2008). Since storytelling is in their DNA (McKee and Gerace 2018), human beings are natural storytellers

S M A Moin, *Brand Storytelling in the Digital Age*,
https://doi.org/10.1007/978-3-030-59085-7_2

(Niles 1999); also known as "homo narrans" (Lund et al. 2018), which refers to "storytelling human". Even in the religious scriptures, including the Qur'an and the Bible, there are many stories told in the words of God. The Qur'an mentions that Almighty God has created human beings and taught them how to narrate stories: "has created man, and has taught him articulate speech" (Qur'an 55: 3–4). Here, man refers to human beings at large.

Over the period, this ancient art has become an essential part of human nature. Serving as an "emotional glue" (Krevolin 2016, p. 74), storytelling differentiates human beings from all other species, giving them incredible power to connect emotionally and foster cooperation (Papadatos 2006). Storytelling has attracted the attention of the marketing researchers for its astonishing power of persuasion (Garmston 2019; Krevolin 2016), covering the areas marketing strategy and tactics, brand philosophy (McKee and Gerace 2018), consumer psychology, and behaviour (Woodside et al. 2007, 2008; Woodside 2010). It also extensively covers the areas of branding, advertising, and sales (McKee and Gerace 2018) including brand promotion, product placement, and the relationship between customers and brands (Woodside 2010), brand DNA (Krevolin 2016), and brand storytelling (McKee and Gerace 2018; Aaker 2018). However, there has been a paradigm shift in the way storytelling has shaped marketing communications, brand marketing, and how marketing views storytelling in the modern-day. The dominant role of storytelling in marketing has evolved from using news stories as vehicles to interrupt the customers and deliver brand and product messages; to using stories as advertising tactics; to developing, managing and delivering the overall brand strategy (McKee and Gerace 2018; Delgado-Ballester and Fernández-Sabiote 2016). Thus, storytelling creates brand engagement, develop brand attachment, and brand affinity. In recent years, research in neuroscience and consumer psychology has contributed to providing scientific evidence behind the power of storytelling to connect with the customers (Plassmann et al. 2012).

However, when it comes to defining this ancient art, in the interdisciplinary literature, there is a tension between two terms: story and narrative. While one school of thought perceives that story and narrative are very different from each other, the other school of thought perceives they are similar. Some researchers consider narrative is a more academic terminology, whereas the story is a casual expression. However, the purpose of the critical review of interdisciplinary literature is not to reconcile this tension, rather reveal the core components of story and narrative that marketers need to understand in order to leverage the ancient art to transform marketing and brand communications in the modern-day. In other words, the insights on storytelling, drawn from various interdisciplinary domains that directly and indirectly intersect the areas of marketing communications and the facets of brand storytelling, will be synthesised in this chapter.

Chronology, Causality, Action, and Consciousness

Delgadillo and Escalas (2004) suggest that story should have at least two elements such as chronology and causality. The chronology dimension of the story suggests that the events within a story take place over a time, which follows Aristotle's universal structure of beginning, middle, and end (Bruner 1990; Escalas 1998). The causality suggests that there should be a cause and effect relationship between the events happening within a story. In the context of marketing communication the scenes, actions, talks, and acts (structural elements) used in a marketing story should have some causal interfacing with the persons (customers), products and brands (Delgadillo and Escalas 2004; Fournier 1998). McKee and Gerace (2018) have given a 3-word definition of the story: "Conflict changes life" (p. 48) and argue that story and narrative are not the same: "All stories are narratives, but not all narratives are stories" (p. 48). However, the narrative theories occupy the majority of the domain of storytelling. The seminal work of McKee (1997) and his recent work with Gerace (2018) focus on the transformation of hero (protagonist), which means the marketing story should tell how customers' lives changes rather than bragging about the product and service features. The same view echoes in Krevolin's (2016) work, defining story as "An engaging character actively overcomes tremendous obstacles to reach a desired goal, and in doing so, the character changes for better" (p. 50).

Bruner (1990) proposes two other essential dimensions of a story, such as the landscape of action and landscape of consciousness. Together these two dimensions allow the audience (readers/viewers) get into the story world. "The landscape of action consists of events that are visible (by sight or imagination) to the casual observer: initiating event, resulting actions, and outcomes. The landscape of consciousness allows the reader/viewer to get inside the head of the story's characters (e.g., protagonist and antagonist)" (Woodside et al. 2008, p. 102).

Emotion, Persuasion, and Narrative Transportation

Many researchers also argue that emotion is a fundamental element of the story (Krevolin 2016; McKee and Gerace 2018). The concept of "evaluative slope" helps in understanding emotion used in the story (Gergen and Gergen 1988). One way of triggering emotion is the art of playing with the unexpected change that breaks the stability of life: the events within a story change the life of the protagonist and capture the attention of the viewers/readers who anxiously wait for restoring stability. "This is what storytellers do. They create moments of unexpected change that seize the attention of their protagonists, and by extension, their readers and viewers. Those who've tried to unravel the secrets of story have long known about the significance of change" (Storr 2019, p. 13). Evaluative slope measures the magnitude of change (Gergen and Gergen 1988)—the degree to which the protagonist's life improves or deteriorates. Steep inclination/declination of the evaluative slope denotes the higher rise and fall and links to the magnitude of emotion (Woodside et al. 2008; Delgadillo and Escalas 2004). Following a traditional approach and linking emotion with two types of arousal: activation and physiological, Berger (2013) has categorised emotions into four types:

1. Positive (pleasant) emotion with high arousal such as awe, excitement, and amusement.
2. Negative (unpleasant) emotion with high arousal, which includes anger and anxiety.
3. Positive (pleasant) emotion with low arousal, such as containment, and
4. Negative (unpleasant) emotion with low arousal, such as sadness.

While existing literature acknowledges the role of emotion in storytelling and marketing, drawing on the empirical data, Berger's (2013) argue that marketers need to understand the role of arousal in order to understand why people share contents. Sharing of content is particularly important in the connected era, which often ends up as customers telling stories, and these become even powerful than marketers telling stories. Berger's (2013) research revealed that the high arousal, whether positive or negative make people share things with others. So, when people feel awe, excitement, amusement, or anger and anxiety, they tend to share. However, they are not inclined to share things when they feel low arousal.

Following the managerial implication of Berger's (2013) research, while using emotion in stories, including brand stories, marketers need to master the art of using high-positive arousal for the protagonist and the high-negative aerosol for the antagonist to trigger more engagement. Emotion also plays an essential role in brand storytelling as customers usually buy through emotion followed by the use of logic to rationalise their decision (Rodriguez 2020).

Drawing on the "narrative transportation theory", researchers have identified storytelling as one of the best ways of pursuing others using both emotion and cognition. Drawing on Green and Brock (2002), Delgado-Ballester and Fernández-Sabiote (2016, p. 120) asserts, "when consumers are transported by (i.e. absorbed or immersed in) the story told, narrative processing predominates over analytical processing." Rodriguez (2020) argues that people digest and remember contents communicated through storytelling more easily due to its superior capability of connecting information and emotion than any other form of communication. Thus, when compared analytical processing, narrative processing of information and brand messages are less critically analysed with fewer arguments and negative thoughts, resulting in more affective responses and enhanced persuasion (Green and Brock 2002).

Experiential Outcome and Moral Sense Making

While emotion is an ingredient of a story that helps in connecting with others, storytelling nurtures the inner feelings, resulting in emotional and moral experiential outcomes. Literature intersecting emotion and storytelling reveals that people can experience "catharsis" by expressing suppressed emotion by telling stories (Woodside et al. 2008; Holt 2003; Jung 1959). Catharsis refers to a deeply experienced feeling, which is more like "proper pleasure" mentioned by Aristotle (Hiltunen 2002). Many people find storytelling as a way of emotional cleansing and purification of our inner selves through sharing a part of our life. Telling personal stories is an art of giving others an open invitation into the storyteller's inner world. Charismatic leaders who are good in storytelling expose their personal life through the art of storytelling to be transparent to their people. Sharing personal stories shorten the distance between the tellers and listeners, connecting them at a deeper level.

Coined by Sanders and van Krieken (2018), the other experiential outcome of moral sense making is Phronesis. Phronesis is related to moral transformation experienced through the struggles of a hero within the story, leading to prudence and practical wisdom. Phronesis is the state of feeling acquired through moral sense making, which empowers the hero to differentiate right from wrong. Triggered by the inward reflection of an individual's moral stance resulting from enacting heroic deeds, someone experiences an ethically awakening experiential feeling, known as Phronesis.

Brain's Response to Storytelling

The research in intersection of neuroscience and consumer psychology have unveiled how brain responds to storytelling (Plassmann et al. 2012), which brought a new dimension in storytelling research. The Triune Brain Model, invented by neuroscientist Paul MacLean in 1960, divides the human brain into three significant parts: reptilian, mammalian, and primate parts. However, the publication of his book, The Triune Brain in Evolution: Role in Paleocerebral Function, in 1990, popularised the concept of Triune Brain Model. The reptilian brain, referred to as the instinctual part, deals with things such as aggression and territory. The mammalian brain, known as the emotional part, handles things like food and sex. The primate brain is the thinking part of the brain and deals with perception, planning, and handling complex concepts and known as the thinking part of the brain. This part of the brain also deals with more profound meaning, helping people to seek the purpose of life.

The other stream of research on the effect of storytelling in the domain of neuroscience focuses on the memory system, understanding how people remember things. This type of research, when intersects with the areas of marketing, consumer psychology, and consumer behaviour provides marketers clues about how consumers remember brands which in turn, lead to the development of appropriate communication strategy and brand storytelling. Bettman (1979) and Tulving (1985) identified memory systems such as procedural, semantic, and episodic, which help in the acquisition and retention of knowledge of the events experienced, allowing someone to travel back. These also provide a fundamental basis for explaining two storytelling principles: story-based memory and episodic memory (Moin et al. 2020). The ***story-based memory*** is concerned about the way of processing information by the brains. Schank (1999) claims, "human memory is story-based" (p. 12). Supporting this claim, Woodside (2010) argues, "information is indexed, stored, and retrieved in the form of stories" (p. 532). Story indices play a significant role in the memorability of the event by the story listener, forming an emotional attachment with them through the use of plots, characters, challenges, quest, and lessons learned. Story indices nurture ***story-based memory and*** help in creating stronger awareness and developing intuitive understanding (Woodside 2010). Singh and Sonnenburg (2012) posit that story can help in creating meaning and develop empathy through the use of location, action, attributes, problems, and characters, helping the consumers embark on an emotional journey. Thus, storytelling has been used as a vehicle to communicate brand messages emotionally (Berger 2013). Singh and Sonnenburg (2012) also argue that the memorability of stories increases as the number of indices increases as it helps the story to reside in more places of the memory, making the recalling easier and better.

The episodic memory, on the other hand, deals with the process of storing and retrieving the memory, built on how human beings remember something. Instead of remembering things through data and facts, human beings have natural inclination to remember things in the form of stories, which includes events, incidents, and experiences (Woodside 2010). In the case of marketing principle, this helps in explaining person-to-person and person-and-brand relationships (Fournier 1998; Schank 1990).

Another body of neuroscience research deals with the different types of hormone released on the human brain, which affect the way they feel and respond. Studies also support that when exposed to stories, several hormones are released: dopamine contributes to feeling (pleasure and satisfaction), cortisol affect a person to act (fight or flight), endorphin causes the feeling of pleasure, and oxytocin associates with empathy, trust, sexual activity and relationship building (Rodriguez 2020). This invaluable information revealed through the development in neuroscience substantiates the need for brand storytelling to affect customers feeling and brand marketers can use this knowledge to design stories to affect their feelings and behaviour, enhancing brand engagement, brand experience, as well as the brand attachment.

Storytelling in Marketing and Consumer Psychology

One of the primary focuses of storytelling in marketing and consumer psychology is how consumers and brands converse (Woodside et al. 2008) and share online and offline product and service consumption experience. Customer-generated marketing is highly potent in the age of social media-driven sharing economy as what customers feel and spread is more potent than what brands claim (McKee and Gerace 2018). Holt and Thompson (2004) vow that consumption experiences are dramatic, having the potential to be a powerful message, wrapped in the word of mouth stories. Nonetheless, marketing, particularly advertising, has embraced storytelling as a tactical tool.

Argument-Based Versus Story-Based Adverting

There is an apparent reason why storytelling has been a popular tool for developing advertising. Woolley (2019) posits that advertisements are failing to capture the attention and interest of consumers. Traditional advertisements have become not only ineffective but also annoying, resulting in a trend of online ad blocking and ad skipping. A survey of 1015 people conducted by ORC International in collaboration with Mirriad, an ad-tech firm, revealed that 76% are blocking ads online and skipping traditional TV ads, while 90% of people skip pre-roll ads (Elkin 2016). According to experts, most of the Americans view around 4000–10,000 ads per day, which creates noise and the messages conveyed fail to capture attention and are not sticking with them. The survey revealed that amongst the adverts seen in the last week, 68% of people could recall less than five (Elkin 2016). Traditional argumentative advertisements, where marketer talk (stay in the active end) and viewers passively receive the message (stay in the passive end) with hardly any opportunity to engage found to be the main reason (Fitzgerald and Arnott 2000). The evolving scenarios of adverts failing to connect with the customers demand a more indirect approach and interactive conversations between the brands and the consumers. In this context, many marketers have used storytelling to transform marketing communication through story-based advertisement where message delivered in an artistic way wrapped with stories. Instead of communicating through a lecture approach, story-based advertisements hook the audience through providing meaning to their life,

creating cognitive and emotional impact and transporting them through the story into an immersive world (Fitzgerald and Arnott 2000). Thus, story-based advertisement dramatically improves the interaction between brands and consumers, resulting in a more positive attitude and sentiment and more dynamic information processing, higher brand recall and purchase intent (Madura and Nowacki 2018). Through creating strong emotional appeal, story-based commercial can pursue customers better than the fact-based and feature-based advertisements and generate a sense of trust (Fitzgerald and Arnott 2000; Yaakop and Brown 2013). Thus, the practice and application of storytelling offer a novel approach to engage with their customers with more and more brands integrating storytelling as an essential part of an advertisement. There has been a shift in marketing communication in the modern-day, which views consumers as the co-creators of marketing contents rather than just consuming them.

Bowling vs. Pinball Marketing

The researchers have metaphorically explained the shift in marketing as a shift from the bowling game to pinball game (Singh and Sonnenburg 2012; Henning-Thurau et al. 2013).

In the traditional bowling-marketing, marketer leverage the use of all marketing instruments to craft the best message (the ball), playing a reasonably consistent game on the predictable runway. Success depends on marketers ability to reach the message (the ball) to the intended customers (the pins). However, in the contemporary pinball game, the brand message (the ball) is co-created by brand managers and customers in a more dynamic social media-enabled virtual environment. Thus the content (pinball) crafted by the marketers and consumed by the customers; instead, co-created while shared between customers (bounce bars). The success of a pinball marketing game is less predictable, and marketers have less control over the outcome of the game (Hennig-Thurau et al. 2010; Muñiz and Schau 2007). In the age of social media, the pinball game played mostly in terms of brand storytelling due to its incredible power to bind consumers both intellectually and emotionally with consumers playing a more active role to tell the brand stories (Singh and Sonnenburg 2012) through easy-to-use digital technologies.

Storytelling in Brand Communications

Storytelling has a profound role in attaching meaning to brands. People are often fascinated to brands rather than products as brands give them the meaning in the form of the stories that they tell to themselves and others. A good body of research originating from the domains of consumer psychology and psychoanalytic research on branding (Woodside et al. 2008) also view a brand as an icon or archetype, seeing it with its anthropomorphic identities (Fournier 1998; Hirschman 2000; Holt 2003). An archetype brings brands to life by creating an emotional feeling with consumers for the protagonist. Brand storytelling theories coupled with the archetypal theories advance the practice of "*brand mediated archetype enactment*" (Moin et al. 2020), central to which is the perception that consumers can form a relationship with brands (Fournier 1998). Archetypes bring brands from the boundaries of the organisations into the consumer world, allowing them to experience and feel happiness or concern through imagining them with specific plots "that people need help in finding what makes them happy, and this is where marketing comes in" (Bagozzi and Nataraajan 2000, p. 10) with stories, characters, emotions, and logic. The seminal work of Fournier (1998) identified fifteen facets of brand–consumer relationships, giving marketers a wide range of avenues to connect with their customers and develop brand–consumer relationships. The archetype theory was originated by Jung (1959) and further promoted by Campbell (1949) with the concept of the hero's journey. The concept and essence of the hero's journey, widely used by movies, brand commercials, and brand promotional videos, dramatised the ways of inviting viewers and customers on a transformational journey. Moin et al. (2020) have critically examined the narrative structure and art of storytelling used by the destination brands, finding the scope for improving the way brands tell stories in their communications. While applying the archetypical theories, often brands make a mistake by adopting the role of hero. This approach mostly fails as customers—not the brand—are at the centre of brand storytelling (Rodriguez 2020) and are the heroes of the brand stories. Donald (2017) posits that brands should ideally play the role of a guide who can identify the customer's (protagonist) problems and give them a plan to overcome those challenges. Brands should assume the role of Yoda while considering their customers as the Luke Skywalker in Star Wars (Donald 2017).

Seeking Clarity, and Communicating Values

The brand personality theories (Aaker 1997) associate human attributes with brands, making brands livelier and a significant part of the consumers' lives. Like DNA differentiates human from each other, brand DNA determines what the brand stands for, differentiating one brand from the others. However, there is a need for a vessel that can carry the brand meaning. Stories are the vessels that carry the message (Berger 2013), creating meaning in the lives of the customers.

Since storytelling has been an integral part of human identity and social fabric, telling stories helps people discover their identity and seeking clarity (Woodside 2010; Weick 1995). Drawing on neuroscience, psychology and evolutionary biology, Gottschall (2012) revealed that storytelling plays a vital role in making us human. Through stories, people invite others into their inner world; get connected with others at a deeper level and form camaraderie. In the branding context, marketers use brand stories to create and communicate brand meaning and brand values to those consumers who love to share similar values and find brand stories as a way of telling their own stories. Brands became a vessel for them to express themselves: "Brand storytelling isn't about creating marketing campaigns but building tribes and inspiring movements (Walter and Gioglio 2019, p. 3). Brand stories have profound implications in transformational tourism that attract people to seek meaning for their lives while travelling the world and gathering stories. Often these stories become the vehicle to discover themselves—they can feel their pulse and hear their voice while sharing their stories with others as Weick (1995) says: "How do I know what I think until I hear what I say?" (Woodside 2010, p. 533).

Approaches to Branding and Associated Storytelling

Heding et al. (2016) have identified seven approaches to brand management research drawing on many philosophical, academic, and scientific traditions: economic, identity, consumer-based, personality, relational, community and cultural approaches to branding. Critical evaluation of these approaches can contribute to the understanding of different types of brand storytelling.

Economic Approach: Brand the Hero

The branding research was influenced by economics before 1985, leading to economic approaches to branding, which views consumers as an economic man. As the economic man makes rational choices while choosing and consuming brands, and driven by utility maximisation, consumption viewed as linear and transactional. Therefore, the idea of brand management under economic approach was to manipulate the "marketing mix" (Borden 1964), and the brand storytelling mainly used a product-centric rhetorical storytelling approach to communicate the superior product quality using criteria related to features and functionality, portraying brand as the hero or icon.

Identity Approach: Organisation the Hero

The identity approach, shifting the focus from the product-level to organisational-level, became popular around the mid-90s with the assumption that brand needs to have a unified and coherent identity—both internally to employees and externally to customers, which became the focal point for brand value creation (Hatch and Schultz 1997). Brand storytelling centred on organisational behaviour, promoting the organisational values and affecting the organisational identity, image, and reputation. Thus, the purpose-driven storytelling focusing on the brand DNA (Krevolin 2016), communicating why the brand exists and the core values, viewing the organisation as the hero or icon.

Consumer-Based Approach: Customer the Hero

Another remarkable shift in the thinking of brand management, led by the new article on customer-based brand equity by Keller (1993) marked the beginning of the consumer-based approach. The consumer-based approach treats brands as cognitive construal, assuming that brands reside in the minds of the consumers. Therefore, the brand prophecy is that consumers own the brand and controls the value creation. Significantly different from the economic and the identity approaches to branding, which primarily focus on the sending end of brand communication, the consumer-based approach views consumers as the owner of the brand. With an outside-in approach, the brand storytelling focused on customers, viewing them as the hero or protagonist while the brand plays the role of a mentor (supportive role). Nonetheless, following the same analogy that a programmer can control a computer, the marketers were still in control of crafting and telling the brand stories to incite more word of mouth marketing and consumer-to-consumer storytelling (Heding et al. 2016).

Personality Approach: Customer the Hero

Drawing on human psychology, personality research and consumer behaviour, in 1997, Aaker's (1997) publication on brand personality dimensions, popularised the personality approach to branding. The personality approach assumes that a brand can be viewed as a living entity so consumers can ascribe personality to a brand, and focuses on how and why people choose brands with certain personalities (Aaker 1997)—in other words, how personality makes a difference (Plummer 1985). Brand personality refers to "the set of human characteristics associated with a brand" (Aaker 1997, p. 347), assumed to be enduring, distinct and stable. The key to brand consumption shifted from the functionality of the products to how the products help the customers to express themselves. The brand storytelling focused on the symbolic meaning brands create in the lives of their consumers rather than promoting the physical and functional characteristics of the products. Creating an emotional bonding between brand and consumers was the primary aim of the brand stories, encouraging consumers to use brands to tell the story of who they are and what they stand for. Customers are still the heroes, but the brand provides symbolic meaning to their lives.

Relational Approaches: Customer the Hero

In 1998, through her seminal work, "*Consumers and Their Brands: Developing relationship theory in consumer research*," published in the *Journal of Consumer Research*, Susan Fournier introduced a new way of looking at the brand-consumer relationship. This marks a new beginning of relational approaches to branding and assumes that consumers can also experience relationships with brands as they experience relationships among themselves. The relational approach assumes that brand meaning is created through the process of dyadic and cyclical brand–consumer exchange, resembling human relationships. Consumers remain at the centre of brand storytelling, playing the protagonist role. The relational brand storytelling focus on consumers-brand engagement that foster at least fifteen facets of relationships, still viewing customers the heroes who also own the brand and act as an active part of the creation of meaning.

Community Approach: Brand Tribe the Hero

Popularised in 2001, the community approach to branding began with the evolution of a social community centred on a brand, known as a brand tribe (Muñiz and O'Guinn 2001). Different from personality and the relational approach where the brand value was co-created through the dialogue between marketers and consumers (dyadic relationship), the community approach found meaning through social interaction among brand tribes (triadic relationship). Brand tribes are dedicated consumers who share the same values as the brand. In this approach, the brand storytelling made a sharp turn from marketers telling stories to brand tribes telling stories (Muñiz and Schau 2007), which is far more powerful and effective (Walter and Gioglio 2019).

Cultural Approach: Brand the Storyteller

The cultural approach focuses on the role of a brand within a culture where the brand is seen as a "cultural artefact moving through history" (Holt 2004, p. 215). Unlike identity approach, the cultural approach is interested in consumer culture rather than organisational culture. In the cultural approach, the brands are enmeshed into the culture (Holt 2002). How brands and culture influence each other is a critical question. Brand storytelling is shaped by culture, while brands also play an influential role within the culture.

"The brand is a storyteller, endowed with cultural meaning and an important factor in the intricate web of cultural meanings used in the collective identity projects of consumers. In that sense, the brand is a vessel of meaning and myth making, successful only if it resonates with consumers' collective identity projects of the time. Understanding the brand–consumer exchange in the relational approach also requires an understanding of the identity projects of consumers. It is, however, important to note that the understanding and focus of consumers' identity projects is different in the two approaches. In the cultural approach consumers' identity projects are analysed at a (macro) collective level. The relational approach is concerned with the understanding of individual identity projects as important contributors to brand meaning" (Heding et al. 2016, p. 210).

Scale of Measurement

While many researchers provided the definition and elements of a good and well-told story, Escalas's (1998) 6-item 5-point ("1 = not at all" and "5 = very much") scale gives an option to measure it (Woodside et al. 2008) (Table 2.1).

Further to the narrative theories focusing on the practice and application of storytelling are covered in Chapter 5.

Table 2.1 Storytelling: a scale of measurement

Areas of measurement	*Items of measurement*
The main characters' engagement in goals seeking	To what extent do these thoughts consist of actors engaged in actions to achieve goals?
The entry into characters' (particularly the main character's) inner world: hearts and minds	To what extent do these thoughts let you know what the actors are thinking and feeling?
The transformation (change) of the main character	To what extent do these thoughts provide you with insight about the personal evolution or change in the life of a character?
The presence of casualty	To what extent do these thoughts explain why things happen, that is, what caused things to happen?
The story structure	To what extent do these thoughts have a well delineated beginning (initial event), middle (crisis or turning point), and ending (conclusion)?
Balance between specifics and generalizations	To what extent do these thoughts focus on specific, particular events rather than generalizations or abstractions?

Source Adapted from Woodside et al. (2008, pp. 102–103)

Storytelling in Tourism and Destination Marketing

Storytelling has got significant attention in tourism, and destination marketing with destination organisations (DMOs) that are extensively using the promotional videos to tell brand stories (Youssef et al. 2018; Moin et al. 2020). Storytelling is a great way to bring the destination brands and tourists together on a virtual conversation. Sharing personal transformational stories by the tourist plays a crucial role in word of mouth marketing and promotes advocacy (Chronis 2005; McCabe and Foster 2006). Viewing travelling as consumption of destinations and tourists experiencing multi-sensory memory, brand messages shared through first-hand authentic stories by the consumers become compelling. There is also evidence that the perceptions developed through others' stories disseminated through a range of social media platforms can shape tourists' experience (Gretzel et al. 2006). Wong et al. (2016) have coined this feeling of a virtual journey that shapes our perceptions as imaginative, transporting narratives.

The modern-day commercials have embraced the art of storytelling (Herskovitz and Crystal 2010) as Gallo (2016) argue that stories inform, engage, and inspire—this is true in case of both customer acquisition, customer retention, and repeat purchase. The evocative stories, images and exoticised imaginaries are èfficient ways of destination marketing (Salazar 2012) in the modern-day. Research on storytelling in tourism takes the path of two main streams. The first stream focuses on the experiential stories of the tourists already visited the destinations (Nimrod 2008; Desforges 2000). These are user-generated stories, spread through travel blogs and via social media channels and coined as *customers telling stories* (Moin et al. 2020). These stories can come from two types of customers—one who perceive tourism as a way to escape from the hard routines of regular life; and the one who see travelling as a quest of finding meaning in their lives to fill the spiritual vacuum and feeding their souls, known as transformational tourism (Robledo and Batle 2017; Pearson 1989). The transformational tourism aligns with Campbell's (1949) infamous storytelling framework of Hero's Journey, where a protagonist transforms through overcoming struggles and challenges of the new world. The second research stream focuses on stories told through commercials and other promotional activities created by marketers and creative agencies (Youssef et al. 2018; Lichrou et al. 2010), also coined by Moin et al. (2020) as ***marketers telling stories***. The success depends on the ability to create compelling stories by the marketers that not only attract the attention of the customers but also create a conversation that eventually creates many user-generated stories and work as a vehicle to convey the brand meaning and create an emotional bond between brands and customers.

In summary, drawing on different disciplines, this chapter has given a critical review of the literature on storytelling focusing on brand and marketing communications. For further research in the field of storytelling, an interdisciplinary approach is recommended for an in-depth understanding of the different facets of storytelling, leading to the development of more sound theories. Interdisciplinary insights of storytelling have profound implications in transforming the practices and applications of storytelling.

References

Aaker, D. (2018). *Creating Signature Stories: Strategic Messaging That Energies, Persuades and Inspire*. New York: Morgan James Publishing.

Aaker, J. L. (1997). Dimensions of Brand Personality. *Journal of Marketing Research, 34,* 347–356.

Bagozzi, R., & Nataraajan, R. (2000). The Year 2000: Looking Forward. *Psychology & Marketing, 17,* 1–11.

Berger, J. (2013). *Contagious: How to Build Word of Mouth in the Digital Age*. New York: Simon and Schuster.

Bettman J. R. (1979). Memory Factors in Consumer Choice: A Review. *Journal of Marketing, 43*(Spring), 37–53.

Borden, N. (1964). The Concept of the Marketing Mix. In G. Schwartz (Ed.), *Science in Marketing*. New York: Wiley.

Bruner, J. (1990). *Acts of Meaning*. Cambridge, MA: Harvard Business School Press.

Campbell, J. (1949). *The Hero with a Thousand Faces*. Princeton, NJ: Princeton University Press.

Chronis, A. (2005). Coconstructing Heritage at the Gettysburg Storyscape. *Annals of Tourism Research, 32*(2), 386–406.

Delgadillo, Y., & Escalas, J. E. (2004). Narrative Word of Mouth Communication: Exploring Memory and Attitude Effects of Consumer Storytelling. *Advances in Consumer Research, 31,* 186–192.

Delgado-Ballester, E., & Fernández-Sabiote, E. (2016). Once Upon a Brand": Storytelling Practices by Spanish Brands. *Spanish Journal of Marketing, 20*(2), 115–131.

Desforges, L. (2000). Traveling the World: Identity and Travel Biography. *Annals of Tourism Research, 27*(4), 926–945.

Donald, M. (2017). *Building a Story Brand: Clarify Your Message so Customers Will Listen*. Nashville: HarperCollins Leadership.

Elkin, T. (2016). *Survey Finds 90% of People Skip Pre-Roll Video Ads*. Available at: https://www.mediapost.com/publications/article/277564/survey-finds-90-of-people-skip-pre-roll-video-ads.html. Accessed 25 Mar 2020.

Escalas, J. E. (1998). Advertising Narratives: What Are They and How Do They Work? In B. Stern (Ed.), *Representing Consumers: Voices, Views, and Visions* (pp. 267–289). New York: Routledge.

Fitzgerald, M., & Arnott, D. (2000). *Marketing Communications Classics: An International Collection of Classic and Contemporary Papers*. London: Cengage Learning.

Fournier, S. (1998). Consumers and Their Brands: Developing Relationship Theory in Consumer Research. *Journal of Consumer Research, 24*, 343–374.

Gallo, C. (2016). *The Storyteller's Secret: How TED Speakers and Inspirational Leaders Turn Their Passion into Performance*. London, UK: Macmillan.

Garmston, R. J. (2019). *The Astonishing Power of Storytelling: Leading, Teaching and Transforming in a New Way*. Thousand Oaks, CA: Corwin.

Gergen, K. J., & Gergen, M. M. (1988). Narrative and the Self as Relationship. *Advances in Experimental Social Psychology, 21*, 17–56.

Gottschall, J. (2012). *The Storytelling Animal: How Stories Make Us Human*. New York: Mariner.

Green, M. C., & Brock, T. C. (2002). In the Mind's Eye: Transportation-Imagery Model of Narrative Persuasion. In M. C. Green, J. J. Strange, & T. C. Brock (Eds.), *Narrative Impact: Social and Cognitive Foundations* (pp. 315–341). Mahwah, NJ: Lawrence Erlbaum.

Gretzel, U., Fesenmaier, D. R., & O'Leary, J. T. (2006). The Transformation of Consumer Behaviour. In *Tourism Business Frontiers* (pp. 31–40). Chicago: Routledge.

Hatch, M. J., & Schultz, M. (1997). Relations Between Organizational Culture, Identity and Image. *European Journal of Marketing, 31*(5–6), 356–365.

Heding, T., Knudtzen, C., & Bjerre, M. (2016). *Brand Management: Research, Theory, and Practice*. Abingdon, Oxon: Routledge.

Henning-Thurau, H., Hofacker, C. F., & Bloching, B. (2013). Marketing the Pinball Way: Understanding How Social Media Change the Generation of Value for Consumers and Companies. *Journal of Interactive Marketing, 27*, 237–241.

Hennig-Thurau, T., Malthouse, E. C., Friege, C., Gensler, S., Lobschat, L., Rangaswamy, A., et al. (2010). The Impact of New Media on Customer Relationships. *Journal of Service Research, 13*(3), 311–330.

Herskovitz, S., & Crystal, M. (2010). The essential Brand Persona: Storytelling and Branding. *Journal of Business Strategy, 31*(3), 21–28.

Hiltunen, A. (2002). *Aristotle in Hollywood: The Anatomy of Successful Storytelling*. Bristol, UK: Intellect Books.

Hirschman, E. (2000). Consumers' Use of Intertextuality and Archetypes. *Advances in Consumer Research, 27,* 57–63.

Holt, D. B. (2002, June). Why Do Brands Cause Trouble? A Dialectical Theory of Consumer Culture and Branding. *Journal of Consumer Research, 29,* 70–90.

Holt, D. B. (2003). What Becomes an Icon Most? *Harvard Business Review, 81,* 43–49.

Holt, D. B. (2004). *How Brands Become Icons: The Principles of Cultural Branding*. Boston, MA: Harvard Business School Press.

Holt, D. B., & Thompson, C. J. (2004). Man-of-Action Heroes: The Pursuit of Heroic Masculinity in Everyday Consumption. *Journal of Consumer Research, 31,* 425–440.

Jung, C. G. (1959). The Archetypes and the Collective Unconscious. In H. Read, M. Fordham, & G. Adler (Eds.), *Collected Works* (Vol. 9, p. 1). Princeton, NJ: Princeton University Press (Originally published in 1916).

Kaufman, B. (2003). Stories That Sell, Stories That Tell. *Journal of Business Strategy, 24*(2), 11–15.

Keller, K. L. (1993, January). Conceptualizing, Measuring, and Managing Customer-Based Brand Equity. *Journal of Marketing, 57,* 1–22.

Krevolin, R. (2016). *The Hook: How to Share Your Brand's Unique Story to Engage Customers, Boost Sales, and Achieve Heartfelt Success*. Wayne: The Career Press Inc.

Lichrou, M., O'Malley, L., & Patterson, M. (2010). Narratives of a Tourism Destination: Local Particularities and Their Implications for Place Marketing and Branding. *Place Branding and Public Diplomacy, 6*(2), 134–144.

Lund, N. F., Cohen, S. A., & Scarles, C. (2018, June). The Power of Social Media Storytelling in Destination Branding. *Journal of Destination Marketing & Management, 8,* 271–280.

Madura, B., & Nowacki, R. (2018). Storytelling and Its Impact on Effectiveness of Advertising. In *8th International Conference on Management*. Available at: https://www.researchgate.net/publication/329035582_STORYTELLING_AND_ITS_IMPACT_ON_EFFECTIVENESS_OF_ADVERTISING. Accessed 21 Mar 2020.

McCabe, S., & Foster, C. (2006). The Role and Function of Narrative in Tourist Interaction. *Journal of Tourism & Cultural Change, 4*(3), 194–215.

McKee, R. (1997). *Story: Style, Structure, Substance, and the Principles of Screenwriting*. New York: HarperCollins.

McKee, R., & Gerace, T. (2018). *Storynomics: Story-Driven Marketing in the Post-Advertising World*. York: Methuen.

Moin, S. M. A., Hosany, S., & O'Brien, J. (2020). Storytelling in Destination Brands' Promotional Videos. *Tourism Management Perspective, 34*, 1–12. https://doi.org/10.1016/j.tmp.2020.100639.

Muñiz, A. M., Jr., & O'Guinn, T. C. (2001, March). Brand Community. *Journal of Consumer Research, 27*, 412–431.

Muñiz, A. M., Jr., & Schau, H. J. (2007). Vigilante Marketing and Consumer-Created Communications. *Journal of Advertising, 36*(3), 35–50.

Niles, J. D. (1999). *Homo Narran: The Poetics and Anthropology of Oral Literature*. Philadelphia: University of Pennsylvania Press.

Nimrod, G. (2008). Retirement and Tourism Themes in Retirees' Narratives. *Annals of Tourism Research, 35*(4), 859–878.

Papadatos, C. (2006). The Art of Storytelling: How Loyalty Marketers Can Build Emotional Connections to Their Brands. *Journal of Consumer Marketing, 23*(7), 382–384.

Pearson, C. (1989). *The Hero Within: Six Archetypes We Live By*. San Francisco, CA: Harper and Row.

Plassmann, H., Ramsøy, T. J., & Milosavljevic, M. (2012). Branding the Brain: A Critical Review and Outlook. *Journal of Consumer Psychology, 22*, 18–36.

Plummer, J. (1985). How Personality Makes a Difference. *Journal of Advertising Research, 24*(6), 27–31.

Qur'an: Chapter 55—Surah Ar-Rahman, Verses 3 and 4.

Robledo, M. A., & Batle, J. (2017). Transformational Tourism as a Hero's Journey. *Current Issues in Tourism, 20*(16), 1736–1748.

Rodriguez, M. (2020). *Brand Storytelling: Put Customers at the Heart of Your Brand Story*. London: Kogan Page.

Salazar, N. B. (2012). Tourism Imaginaries: A Conceptual Approach. *Annals of Tourism Research, 39*(2), 863–882.

Sanders, J., & van Krieken, K. (2018). Exploring Narrative Structure and Hero Enactment in Brand Stories. *Frontiers in Psychology, 9*, 1–17.

Schank, R. C. (1990). *Tell Me a Story: A New Look at Real and Artificial Memory*. New York: Charles Scribner's Sons.

Schank, R. C. (1999). *Dynamic Memory Revisited*. Cambridge: Cambridge University Press.

Singh, S., & Sonnenburg, S. (2012). Brand Performance in Social Media. *Journal of Interactive Marketing, 26*, 189–197.

Storr, W. (2019). *The Science of Storytelling*. London: William Collins.

Tulving, E. (1985). How Many Memory Systems Are There? *American Psychologist, 40*, 385–398.

Walter, E., & Gioglio, J. (2019). *The Laws of Brand Storytelling: Win—and Keep—Your Customers' Hearts and Mind*. New York: McGraw-Hill.

Weick, K. E. (1995). *Sensemaking in Organizations*. Thousand Oaks, CA: Sage.

Wong, J. Y., Lee, S. J., & Lee, W. H. (2016). 'Does It Really Affect Me?' Tourism Destination Narratives, Destination Image, and the Intention to Visit: Examining the Moderating Effect of Narrative Transportation. *International Journal of Tourism Research, 18*(5), 458–468.

Woodside, A. G. (2010). Brand-Consumer Storytelling Theory and Research: Introduction to a Psychology & Marketing Special Issue. *Psychology & Marketing, 27*(6), 531–540.

Woodside, A. G., Krauss, E., Caldwell, M., & Chebat, J.-C. (2007). Advancing Theory for Understanding Travelers' Own Explanations of Discretionary Travel Behavior. *Journal of Travel & Tourism Marketing, 22*, 15–35.

Woodside, A. G., Sood, S., & Miller, K. (2008). When Consumers and Brands Talk: Storytelling Theory and Research in Psychology and Marketing. *Psychology and Marketing, 25*(2), 97–145.

Woolley, D. (2019). What Type of Trust Have We Lost in Media, Marketing and Advertising? *The Drum*. Available at: https://www.thedrum.com/opinion/2019/10/15/what-type-trust-have-we-lost-media-marketing-and-advertising. Accessed 25 Mar 2020.

Worth, S. E. (2008). Storytelling and Narrative Knowing: An Examination of the Epistemic Benefits of Well-Told Stories. *Journal of Aesthetic Education, 42*(3), 42–56.

Yaakop, A., & Brown, J. (2013). Hedonic Pleasure and Social Image: The Effectiveness of Internet Advertising. *Asian Social Science, 9*(1), 179–192.

Youssef, K. B., Leichtb, T., & Marongiuc, L. (2018). Storytelling in the Context of Destination Marketing: An Analysis of Conceptualisations and Impact Measurement. *Journal of Strategic Marketing, 26*(2), 1–18.

CHAPTER 3

Storytelling for Minds: Neuroscience's Approaches to Branding

Abstract Drawing on the science of storytelling and its impact on our brains—explained by studies in the field of neuroscience and two types of thinking—fast and slow—this chapter explores how consumers think while making brand choices and explains three laws drawing on neurosciences approaches to branding. The chapter also explains how stories make biochemical changes in consumers' brains and influence their psychology and behaviour; and how marketers harness storytelling to affect consumers and drive their emotions. Several examples and case studies underline these behaviours.

Keywords Perceived reality versus reality · Thinking fast and slow · Relevance, coherence, and participation · Relevance versus preference

The interdisciplinary research on branding gets a new dimension through the birth of consumer neuroscience (Plassmann et al. 2012), providing a variety of benefits in the study of consumer psychology and brand psychology (Ariely and Berns 2010; Kenning and Plassmann 2008; Lee et al. 2007; Plassmann et al. 2007). The research on brand storytelling, especially in the modern-day, is not complete without understanding how stories influence our brains due to the advancement in neuroscience and our ever-increasing interests into the minds of humankind. As humankind, we are hard-wired with stories, and it is what makes

S M A Moin, *Brand Storytelling in the Digital Age*,
https://doi.org/10.1007/978-3-030-59085-7_3

us human (Corn 2012; Gottschall 2012). The narrative theories and the studies of cognitive psychology, consumer psychology, and brand psychology substantiate the astonishing power of storytelling (Garmston 2019), facilitating brand–consumer conversations (Woodside et al. 2008) and consumers' bonding with brands and shaping the language of brand communication (Krevolin 2016). Neuroscience research, particularly in the last two decades, has also provided substantial evidence on how stories make biochemical changes in our brains. The findings of these studies have profound implications in understanding the role of brand storytelling to engage with modern-day consumers who live in a noisy world (Biesenbach 2018). There are several reasons why consumer neuroscience, where neuroscience intersects with consumer psychology, has reshaped research in the field of branding and consumer behaviour. First, it has drawn valuable insights from neuroscience into the study of consumers. Second, it has contributed to the development of neuro-psychologically sound theory by adopting theories, methods, and approaches from the domain of neuroscience in designing advanced research to understand consumer behaviour.

Neuroscience's study of the nervous system, particularly the areas of complex brain systems are crucial for understanding how story influence consumer biology and how biology influence behaviour. However, not all stories influence consumer behaviour positively. The study on the science of storytelling (Storr 2019) unveils the secrets that can make brands interact and engage with the consumers through storytelling. Drawing on several studies in the field of neuroscience, which intersects the area of storytelling, this chapter reveals how stories impact certain parts of our brains, influence consumer interactions with brands, and how consumers think while making brand choices. The main contribution lies at the intersection of consumer psychology, brand psychology, and interdisciplinary research on brand storytelling and neuroscience. The managerial contributions include insights to the practitioners on the rationale of storytelling and deconstructing storytelling strategies and tactics. The contents of this chapter will also help practitioners to develop compelling brand stories to capture consumers' attention and to engage with them effectively.

Storytelling: The Perspectives of Neuroscience

By nature, our survival as human species depends on the cooperation of bonding and belonging (Jiwa 2019). Neuroscience reveals that storytelling serves this higher purpose of survival and progression through promoting mutual collaborations, which also makes us human (Corn 2012). There are several studies in the field of neuroscience, providing evidence that stories have the power to affect our brains biologically, which in turn affects our psychology, behaviour (Garmston 2019; Zak 2013, 2014, 2015) and decision-making (Damasio 2005). In our brain, there is a part called "amygdala," known as "emotional centre" as it filters the incoming signals to our brain and stimulates our response (Jiwa 2019). Research conducted by Zak (2014) found that hearing of a good story could cause changes in brain activity through the release of oxytocin. Oxytocin is a neurochemical produced in the brain bloodstream when someone listens or watches compelling stories. Neuroscientists have found that oxytocin has a profound effect on our behaviour. Oxytocin enhances our disposition to trust others, making us cooperate while enabling us to experience others' emotions (Garmston 2019). Zak (2014) has also termed it as "*bonding chemical or empathy chemical*," for it enhances a cooperative behaviour to help others.

Several studies found that reading good and humanistic stories promote heightened connectivity in the brains of the readers due to the increased level of oxytocin production and cortisol in the bloodstream, tested by taking a blood sample of the subjects before and after reading stories (Garmston 2019). While oxytocin enhances empathy and positive response, cortisol has the properties to reduce negative responses where the cumulative effects cause broader cooperation (Liberman 2013): found by a study asking the subjects to donate. Table 3.1 shows different hormonal exudation in the brain caused by emotional and compelling stories and their effect on our behavioural attitude.

Table 3.1 Hormonal exudation in the brain caused by stories

Hormones released	*Creates*	*Changes in behavioural attitudes*
Dopamine	Feelings of pleasure	Positive response, to cooperate
Cortisol (stress hormone)	Stress or sense of urgency	To act: fight or flight
Endorphins	Feelings of pleasure	Positive response, to cooperate
Oxytocin (love hormone)	Empathy, trust, sexual desire, and relationship-building	Enhance our disposition to trust and cooperate, trigger emotional response

Source Adapted from Rodriguez (2020, p. 8), Garmston (2019), and Jiwa (2019)

Neuroscience's Approaches to Branding

Neuroscience's approaches to branding supported by scientific research on how consumers think and make choices on the conscious and subconscious level justify why marketers need to engage with their customers through telling the right stories and tell them in the right way. The studies suggest that many brand communications fail to achieve the desired objectives by failing to understand the subtle difference between "reality" and "perceived reality." Walvis (2010) has identified several reasons that explain why and where branding gets wrong, drawing on the perspective of neuroscience (Table 3.2).

Walvis (2010) explained how people think while making various decisions including choosing the brands. The essence of Walvis's (2010) argument aligns with the essence of Kahneman's (2011) seminal work, *Thinking Fast and Slow*. People use slow thinking (Type 2) for tasks demanding analyses and the making of careful choices (e.g. taking tests and filling out a questionnaire). In contrast, they use fast thinking (Type 2) for tasks involving day-to-day routine decision-making. People use their conscious brain while thinking slowly but the subconscious mind while thinking fast. In his book, *Branding with Brain*, Walvis (2010) also highlights that most of the decisions happen in the sub-conscious brain.

Drawing on neuroscience's research, Walvis (2010) argues that the choice of the brands by the consumers follows a process. He has coined it as the "brand-choice algorithm" of the brain and explained the way it functions. The "brand-choice algorithm" is a metaphor that demonstrates that our brain works more like the Google search engine. People usually

Table 3.2 Where branding goes wrong

Denominator	*The perceived reality*	*The reality*
Brand choice	Marketers perceive that customers make brand choices consciously and deliberately	Customers' brand choices happen in the subconscious mind
Consumer behaviour	Marketers perceive that customers are irrational, emotional creatures, and they make brand choices irrationally, entirely driven by emotion	Customers are both emotional and goal-driven. The brain subconsciously makes rational choices. Thus, customers choose brands that are congruent with their personal goals and connect with them emotionally
Product launch	Inconsistent product launching does not have any detrimental effect on brands	There are severe consequences of inconsistent products launching on brands, making people confused about the brand positioning
Brand communication	Reaching as many people as possible matters most	It is not the number of customers rather the quality of the engagement with them matters the most
Marketing communication game	The bowling game of marketing takes precedence over the pinball game of marketing	The pinball game of marketing takes precedence over the bowling game of marketing

Source Adapted from Walvis (2010) and Henning-Thurau et al. (2013)

select brands that tend to serve their current purpose best. These include reminding of their goals, aligning with their meaning, and engaging with them most often in the past. Drawing on neuroscience's position of how people think and choose a brand, Walvis (2010) has deduced three laws of branding: Law of Relevance, Law of Coherence, and Law of Participation. These laws convey profound insights for brand marketers.

Law of Relevance

The relevance law is about focus and suggests that the more uniquely relevant is a branding effort, the higher the chance that the brain will choose it. Therefore, relevance law of branding stresses on "focus", which also aligns with Michael Porter's one of the generic strategies. The more uniquely a brand positions itself, the better it will communicate with the relevant target customers.

> A brand is the tip of an iceberg. How big and how deep the iceberg is will determine how powerful the brand is. The iceberg is the category. If it melts, the brand will melt too. (Ries 2007, online)

By category, Ries (2007) points to brand relevance, citing several examples: Kodak, Red Bull, Starbucks, Marlboro, and Coca Cola. Once known for the world's best film-photography brand, Kodak has fallen in brand value and position on Interbrand ranking as it lost its relevance, and its film-photography iceberg started melting as digital photography started replacing the film-photography. Walvis (2010) argues that the brands that are highly relevant and focus on one thing are linked to the dopamine or reward system in the brain and preferred over other brands by relevant groups of customers. An example is the Volkswagen brand. When people think about safety and automobile, possibly what comes to their mind is Volkswagen, as people want to buy categories but use the brand name as a means to an end, Ries (2007) argues.

Case Study 3.1: Friday by Rebecca Black

In 2011, Rebecca Black, a school-going US girl became viral through the release of her first debut single on YouTube. She was only thirteen years old at that time, and according to many music critics, it was one of the worst songs ever (Berger 2013). Despite, such bad comments by the critics, millions of people listened to the song. As of 6 July 2020, it had 144,339,859 views, 1.1M likes and 3.7M dislikes on YouTube. The song was written and produced by ARK Music Factory based in Los Angeles. The theme of the song was on teenager's life, and joys brought by the coming weekend. The song starts with the brief description of the various days of the week: Sunday (Study, study, study), Monday (Test day), Tuesday (More homework), Wednesday (Music practice), Thursday (Essay due). Then the song captures busy morning routines starting at 7 a.m.

with waking up, freshen up, and taking cereals, rushing to the bus stop. Then, as she gets in the car with her friends on Friday morning (Hooray! Yes! Finally!), everyone starts celebrating the happiness it brings for the weekend feeding and parting.

Although sounding like a monologue of random thoughts, the song becomes one of the most viral videos in 2011 with more than 300 million views on YouTube alone (Berger 2013). While many people were surprised with this astounding success, Professor Jonah Berger, along with his research team at the Warton Business School, revealed the secret. They noticed a pattern of viewership, which gradually rises at the weekdays roll on and the spike on every Friday. Berger (2013) calls it the "Trigger" effect, which is one of the reasons why people share something with others and why things become viral: "Triggers and cues lead people to talk, choose, and use. Social currency gets people talking, but triggers keep them talking. Top of mind means tip of tongue" (p. 92).

Despite the poor quality, the song became viral as it contextualised with Friday, for which many people wait throughout the week. As trigger becomes thing to the top of the mind, it can be explained by the branding law of relevance.

Reflective Questions

1. Explain the astounding success of Rebecca Black's song, Friday through the law of relevance.
2. Find a commercial that uses the same concept of the trigger? What is the trigger, and how it relates to the target consumers? Did the commercial become viral? What was the effect on brand choice by the consumers?

Note: Friday by Rebecca Black commercial is available on https://www.youtube.com/watch?v=kfVsfOSbJY0.

Law of Coherence

The coherence law suggests that the more the marketers coordinate the branding efforts across time and space, the higher the chance for the brain to choose the brand. This calls of the actions of the marketers towards more integrated marketing communications, requiring brands to send messages conveying a unified meaning through all brand channels and all brand touch points throughout the year. The *Law of Coherence* helps in clarifying brand positioning and promoting what brands stand for. More coherent brand messages also help in forming positive emotions with us. Brands should provide coherent brand messages and experience through all brand touchpoints. This is why some luxury fashion brands prefer to destroy unsold goods rather than putting them on sale. This saves them from the trap of short-term profitability, maintaining brand positioning. We find that while Apple launches a new product, the current CEO, Tim Cook, follows the same style of Steve Jobs. This gives customers a coherent message. Failing to do so may cost a fortune to companies which can be substantiated with several examples.

Law of Participation

Draws on brand engagement theories, the law of participation suggests that the more the interactions between the customers and the brand, the higher the chance that the brain algorithm will select the brand. "Share a Coke", first launched in Australia, in 2011, is one of the hugely successful campaigns. The campaign encouraged people to share a Coke with their friends and family members with an innovative idea. As part of this campaign, Coca Cola printed 150 most popular names onto millions of bottles and cans. A compelling commercial, aimed at creating a more personal relationship with the consumers, fostering brand engagement by inspiring consumers to share their moments of happiness by sharing a coke with loved ones with their names written on it. This idea became so welcoming to Australians that other countries around the world adopted it. Instead of first names, China printed nicknames, providing more personalisation. The 2016-campaign in the USA became extremely popular with "Share a Coke and a Song" with popular song lyrics printed on the bottles. In 2017, the UK campaign printed more than 75 holiday destinations. However, the bottles with popular names were available in the store. Customers had the opportunity to order their personalised coke online with the names they wanted. One of the reasons behind the success of this campaign is its ability to foster engagement between customers. However, this campaign also supports the manifestation of "The Law of Relevance".

Battles in Consumers' Mind: Relevance Versus Preference

In the age of information and hyper-competition, getting consumer attention is a big challenge for the brands. Everyday consumers experience information overload. In regards to making a brand choice, the neuroscience's approaches to branding suggest that two kinds of battles take place in consumers' mind: the relevance and the preference battles (Walvis 2010) while going through a three-stage process of decision-making.

The Relevance Battle

The first battle is the relevance battle. The law of relevance suggests that brands have to be relevant in the minds of the customers, focusing on their needs. A buying process starts with problem recognition. In this stage, consumers identify their needs. Once need is identified, they begin the information search when the relevance battle begins. The battle takes place in the minds of the consumers as they develop the consideration set of relevant brands that are better aligned with their needs. For example, a customer looking for a sport utility vehicle is likely to consider brands like Lexus, BMW, and Cadillac while unlikely to choose brands like Roll-Royce, Bentley, and Porsche brands. Therefore, to match customers' needs, the brand should be relevant. The brands that fail to reflect customers' needs will be out in the battle for relevance. The winning in the relevance battle is ascertained to brands if customers do not consider the competing brands. Ries (2007) claims that successful branding strategy should first focus on the category to survive in the relevance battle. Thus, brands should focus on disruptive or radical innovation to create an absolutely new category or sub-category so that the competitors' brands become irrelevant. This also reflects the blue-ocean strategy. The relevance battle is comparatively less competitive and less price sensitive. As the brand strategy is to be different rather than being better, the relevance is less competitive where competing brands do not target the same segments.

The Preference Battle

The brands that survive the relevance battle go through the next battle, known as preference battle, in the mind of the consumers. At this stage, consumers look for the brands that offer them the highest functional and psychological value for their money, time and effort in the acquisition of the brand. Preference of the brand determines the winning of the battle in this stage. To win in this battle, brands adopt incremental innovation and a strategy to be better and cheaper than the competing brands. There is fierce competition in this battle and very hard to win.

To summarise, advancement in the field of neuroscience has provided scientific proofs on how the power of storytelling affects our brain by releasing certain hormones and influence our behavioural response. Neuroscience's approaches to branding and its discovery of how consumers think while making brand choices provides invaluable insights to practitioners. Research at the intersection of neuroscience, consumer psychology, and brand storytelling is an area that demands further investigation with the potential to advance the field and shape the future of storytelling.

References

Ariely, D., & Berns, G. S. (2010). Neuromarketing: The Hope and Hype of Neuroimaging in Business. *Nature Reviews Neuroscience, 11*(4), 284–292.

Berger, J. (2013). *Contagious: How to Build Word of Mouth in the Digital Age*. New York: Simon and Schuster.

Biesenbach, R. (2018). *Unleash the Power of Storytelling: Win Hearts, Change Minds, Get Results*. Orrington Ave, Evanston: Eastlawn Media.

Corn, L. (2012). *Wired for Story: The Writer's Guide to Using Brain Science to Hook Readers from the Very First Sentence*. Berkeley: Ten Speed Press.

Damasio, A. R. (2005). *Descartes' Error: Emotion, Reason, and the Human Brain*. New York: Penguin.

Garmston, R. J. (2019). *The Astonishing Power of Storytelling: Leading, Teaching and Transforming in a New Way*. Thousand Oaks, CA: Corwin.

Gottschall, J. (2012). *The Storytelling Animal: How Stories Make Us Human*. New York: Mariner.

Henning-Thurau, H., Hofacker, C. F., & Bloching, B. (2013). Marketing the Pinball Way: Understanding How Social Media Change the Generation of Value for Consumers and Companies. *Journal of Interactive Marketing, 27*, 237–241.

Jiwa, B. (2019). *The Right Story: A Brief Guide to Changing the World*. Australia: Perceptive Press. https://www.amazon.co.uk/Right-Story-brief-guide-changing/dp/0994432828/ref=sr_1_1?dchild=1&keywords=The+Right+Story%3A+A+Brief+Guide+to+Changing+the+World&qid=1602796025&s=books&sr=1-1.

Kahneman, D. (2011). *Thinking Fast and Slow*. London: Penguin Books.

Kenning, P. H., & Plassmann, H. (2008). How Neuroscience Can Inform Consumer Research. *IEEE Transactionson Neural Systems and Rehabilitation Engineering, 16*(6), 532–538.

Krevolin, R. (2016). *The Hook: How to Share Your Brand's Unique Story to Engage Customers, Boost Sales, and Achieve Heartfelt Success*. Wayne: The Career Press Inc.

Lee, N., Broderick, A. J., & Chamberlain, L. (2007). What Is 'Neuro Marketing'? A Discussion and Agenda for Future Research. *International Journal of Psychophysiology, 63*(2), 199–204.

Liberman, M. (2013). *Social: Why Our Brains Are Wired to Connect*. New York: Crown.

Plassmann, H., Ambler, T., Braeutigam, S., & Kenning, P. (2007). What Can Advertisers Learn from Neuroscience? *International Journal of Advertising, 26*(2), 151–175.

Plassmann, H., Ramsøy, T. J., & Milosavljevic, M. (2012). Branding the Brain: A Critical Review and Outlook. *Journal of Consumer Psychology, 22,* 18–36.

Rebecca Black—Friday (Song on YouTube). Available at: https://www.youtube.com/watch?v=kfVsfOSbJY0.

Ries, A. (2007). *Think Category First, Brand Second, AdAge*. Available at: https://adage.com/article/al-ries/category-brand/120978. Accessed 2 Mar 2020.

Rodriguez, M. (2020). *Brand Storytelling: Put Customers at the Heart of Your Brand Story*. London: Kogan Page.

Storr, W. (2019). *The Science of Storytelling*. London: William Collins.

Walvis, T. (2010). *Branding with Brains: The Science of Getting Customers to Choose Your Company*. Harlow: Pearson Education.

Woodside, A. G., Sood, S., & Miller, K. (2008). When Consumers and Brands Talk: Storytelling Theory and Research in Psychology and Marketing. *Psychology and Marketing, 25*(2), 97–145.

Zak, P. J. (2013). How Stories Change the Brain. *Greater Good Magazine*, Greater Good Science Center at UC Berkeley. Available at: https://greatergood.berkeley.edu/article/item/how_stories_change_brain. Accessed 1 Mar 2020.

Zak, P. J. (2014, October 28). Why Your Brain Loves Good Storytelling. *Harvard Business Review*. Available at: https://hbr.org/2014/10/why-your-brain-loves-good-storytelling. Accessed 12 Dec 2019.

Zak, P. J. (2015). Why Inspiring Stories Make Us React: The Neuroscience of Narrative. *Cerebrum, 2 (PMID: 26034526)*. Available at: https://www.ncbi.nlm.nih.gov/pmc/articles/PMC4445577/. Accessed 6 Mar 2020.

CHAPTER 4

Storytelling for Hearts: Brand–Consumer Conversations in the Digital Age

Abstract Drawing on research associated with emotion, persuasion, and the constructivist brand paradigm, this chapter focuses on the practices of brand storytelling that fosters brand–consumer conversations in the digital age. While explaining different brand stories such as strategic and tactical, the chapter also covers the art of brand storytelling that inspires, influences, and engages consumers.

Keywords Emotional glue · Strategic brand story · Tactical brand story · Emotional hook · Emotional brand values

Who has not heard the stories of Helen of Troy and the wooden horse of the Trojan War? Although most of us have listened to these stories, there are differences in the way we know them. People told these ancient stories uncountable times and in uncountable ways, giving marketers a pearl of wisdom that brand message is communicated better through stories than data (Berger 2013). The ancient art of storytelling is not irrelevant in the modern-day; rather, the influence of social media and the advancement of digital technologies have transformed the art of storytelling.

Storytelling is the new currency of marketing and a strategic asset for the brands and the companies (Aaker 2018). Stories matter because they create meaning and emotionally connect with the consumers. Research conducted at Princeton University found that storytelling affects the

S M A Moin, *Brand Storytelling in the Digital Age*,
https://doi.org/10.1007/978-3-030-59085-7_4

brains of the storytellers and the story-listeners work in the same way and connected by emotional coupling (Gallo 2016). Stories are unforgettable, which makes storytelling an excellent marketing tool for effective brand communication. Although the scientists claim that the world consists of atoms, American poet Muriel Rukeyser opines that it is made of stories: "The world is not made of atoms. It is made of stories" (Jiwa 2019, p. 19).

In the modern-day, people are living in an age of information overload, metaphorically identified as a "noisy world" by Biesenbach (2018). Thousands of brand messages are bombarding the lives of consumers. Research claims that an average consumer in the USA has exposed to two thousand to three thousand different types of communication every day, making it far more difficult for the brands to gain customer attention. Stories have the power to cut through the noise and clutter of information overload (Biesenbach 2018; Aaker 2018). Being noticed no longer provides a competitive advantage to brands. Strong and powerful brands differentiate in the market place not by brand awareness but also by creating brand affinity and a brand tribe, which is supported by the community approaches to branding (Muñiz and O'Guinn 2001). Thus, when Apple launches a new product, many customers eagerly await the whole night in front of the Apple stores to get it just a few hours before everyone else. We can see this scenario even happen when Apple releases the new versions of the existing Apple products. These customers, often known as fans, play the role of brand ambassador, bringing the brand stories to life. They also form a brand community, finding their identity by consuming the brands and using brands as vehicles to tell their own stories (Heding et al. 2016).

A story is a powerful tool to communicate brand messages. Berger (2013) claims that story is a vessel, which carries messages and opines that marketers need to create their Trojan horse if they like to communicate their brand messages with impact. Drawing on research studies, Aaker (2013) claims that:

- Stories are up to 22 times more memorable than facts,
- Communications that combine data and stories resonate with audiences both intellectually and emotionally,
- For lasting effect, brands need to persuade both left and right brain of the consumers; in other words, both cognition and emotion.

Because consumers make the brand choices using their emotion and then rationalise their decisions using logic (Elliott and Percy 2007; Rodriguez 2020) the best way for the brands is to influence consumers' minds is by accessing through their hearts (Jiwa 2019). The recent heart-brain neurodynamics research (McCraty 2015), reveals that extensive neural traffic flow from brain to heart: heart sends more neural signals to the brain, calling "heart" as the gateway or entry path into the emotional experience. This research substantiates that the emotional state can alter by neural signals received in the brain from the heart. Thus, the modern-day marketers need to conquer the hearts of their customers before influencing their minds. Many salespeople use the metaphor that the distance between consumers' wallets and their hearts is shorter than the distance between their wallet and their head, highlighting the role of emotion as a powerful ingredient of marketing communication.

Drawing on psychology and consumer physiology, Jiwa (2019) argues that through harnessing the power of storytelling brands can influence the hearts of their consumers and connect with them emotionally. Research by Paul Zak found that stories create a chemical in the brain known as Oxytocin, which is linked to feeling and cause the story listener to cooperate (Biesenbach 2018). The brands that connect with their customers emotionally tell moving, credible, and compelling brand stories (Krevolin 2016) through different communication channels. So, what is a brand story?

Brand Story: What Is It?

Before defining a brand story, it is essential to understand what a story is and why it matters. Bennet and Royle (2004, p. 55) define "story" as a "series of events in a specific order, with a beginning, a middle, and an end." It is full of incidents having a beginning and an end. Stories reflect our lives. People can relate to the story better: transported and absorbed into good stories (Delgado-Ballester and Fernández-Sabiote 2016). Stern (1994) identified three significant elements of a story such as *chronology*, *causality*, and *character development*. Thus, a story should have sequential events including a beginning, middle and end (*chronology*) with relationships between the events (*causality*). On the other hand, Biesenbach (2018, p. 20) defines a story as "character in pursuit of a goal in the face of some challenge or obstacles", focusing on character, goal and challenges. Krevolin's (2016, p. 50) definition supports Biesenbach's (2018) perception of a story: "An engaging character actively overcomes tremendous obstacles to reach a desired goal, and in doing so, the character changes for better." In essence, a story should be a reflection life, played by a character set on a mission to achieve something desperately and committed to going through challenges. Still, the telling should follow a chronological structure of beginning, middle and end where there is a causal relationship between the events. Likewise, a brand story can be defined as sequential events involving engagement between consumers where consumers play a crucial role as protagonist faced with challenges and brand plays the role of a guide, helping the consumers achieve their goals. Krevolin (2016, p. 17) has articulated this well: "A core concept about brand narratives is the understanding that your brand or product must not be the hero of the story you are telling. Instead, your brand or product must be the helpful ally that allows the consumer to reach their goals, to achieve their potential, to become the person that they were meant to be and couldn't be without your product." The brand needs to establish credibility in the hearts and minds of the consumers to be a helpful ally. The brand story plays a significant role in promoting brand's mission and core values that consumers can relate and associate with the functional and emotional benefits of the brands (Delgado-Ballester and Fernández-Sabiote 2016; Fog et al. 2005).

Coined as "emotional glue" (Krevolin 2016), brand storytelling is at the heart of brand communication, especially in the digital age. Brand stories that clarify the brand values—rather than what it sells or how it sells—connect with the customers better. The essence of the brand story is not to provide information about the features and quality of the products instead create and communicate brand meaning that resonates with the customers and forms emotional relationships. According to Walter and Gioglio (2019, p. 4), "Brand storytelling is the art of shaping a company's identity through the use of narrative and storytelling techniques that facilitate an emotional response and establish meaningful connections." Embedded in all forms of marketing communication whether it targets customers, employees or stakeholders, thriving brand stories centre on people, trigger conversations between brands and the consumers (Woodside et al. 2008), and with the employees. Every interaction or conversation a company has with its customers through ads, blogs, websites, tweets, promotional videos, text, email, mail, telephones, and packaging contributes in shaping the brand story of the company (Walter and Gioglio 2019).

Types of Brand Stories

There are several ways great brands tell stories and talk to their customers (Aaker 2018). Based on their purpose, these can be categorised into strategic and tactical stories.

Strategic Brand-Story

Strategic stories are highly effective in explaining the purpose of the organisation—what the brand stands for—and considered as strategic assets for the company. Aaker (2018) has coined it as ***signature story*** and defined it as "an intriguing, authentic, involving narrative that drives or supports a strategic message clarifying or enhancing the brand vision, customer relationship, organizational values and/or business strategy. It provides visibility and energy to brands and persuade and/or inspire employees and/or customers over an extended time" (p. 10). Thus, the strategic or signature story gives a sense of mission to the company and its people, bringing meaning to their life. The strategic story also explains why a brand exists and defines the core philosophy of the business.

Case Study 4.1: The Power of Strategic Story and the Starbucks' Success

The 30th March of 1971 was a special day for the people of Seattle in the USA as the first coffee revolution started outside the home with Starbucks opening its doors. With a brown mermaid logo, Starbucks launched its first store to sell freshly roasted coffee beans. In 1982, a man by the name of Howard Shultz joined Starbucks as Director of Retail Operations and Marketing. Howard, being interested in people, found coffee as a great excuse to connect with them. In 1983, he had a fantastic opportunity to visit Milan, where he experienced an unforgettable coffee culture. He saw people from all walks of life were bonding across coffee tables in front of the coffee shops, making the streets vibrant and a symbol of social cohesion. The moment became an unforgettable memory in the life of Howard. He wanted to bring this lively coffee culture to the USA. Besides his current job where he had limited authority to implement a strategic change, he kept on exploring all opportunities to turn his dream into a reality.

In 1985, as the opportunity knocked on his door, he founded his coffee brand, Il Giornale. As he poured all his passion into the cup of coffee and tried to create a culture that he experienced in Milan, his brand started growing unexpectedly. In 1987, the local investors responded to his dream. Then surprising everyone in the industry, he acquired Starbucks. Starbucks was re-born, starting its journey under the visionary leadership of Howard Schultz. The second wave of coffee revolution stated in America. Within a few years, Starbucks become one of the trusted brands not only in the USA but also outside the American border, creating coffee tribes in different countries. Marketers were curious to discover the secret of Starbucks's success.

They discovered that the success of Starbucks brand was not in the science of making coffee but in the art of telling a timeless story by Howard Schultz that not only inspired the Starbucks' employees across the world but also resonated with its customers. The story was about how Howard Schultz discovered a new way of feeling the rhythm of life with an unforgettable coffee experience in Milan and his passion for bringing this coffee culture to back home, repositioning a new Starbucks as a "third place" between work and home. Not only that, but it also changed the focus on Starbucks's business as Howard Schultz said, "We are not in the coffee business, serving people, we're in the people business serving coffee." Like Starbucks, many great brands use storytelling to bring their mission to life.

Reflective Question

1. Discuss the essence of third place in the success of Starbucks brand?
2. Critically discuss the role of strategic story in communicating the brand purpose.

For example, the story Howard Shultz told about his vivid coffee experience in Milan and his urge to bring this to life, defined Starbucks as a *people business* that serves coffee instead of *a coffee business* that serves people. Drawing on his golden triangle model, Sinek (2009) explained that most of the companies know *what they do*, some businesses understand *how they do it, while* only a few businesses have clarity about *why they do it*. The strategic stories help brands to clarify the "why" of their business, which ultimately resonates with their employees and the customers who live the same values. The strategic stories, when drawn from the life of the founders and employees can also exemplify what the company does, its values and strategies, target customers, value proposition, and point of difference (Aaker 2018). For instance, when asked about what Harley-Davidson sells, one of the executives answered: "What we sell is the ability for a 43-year old accountant to dress in black leather, ride through small towns and have people be afraid of him" (Walvis 2010, p. 6). The primary sources of the strategic stories are the founder's story behind creating a company or a brand, but it can come from the employees and the customers.

Tactical Brand-Story

In contrast to strategic stories, the tactical stories told through commercials, brand promotional videos, websites and other means of communication are more dynamic and change very often to suit time, offerings and be relevant. Tactical stories are designed to achieve the short-term communication goal of the organisations (Aaker 2018) and are often changed based on brands current needs. The two of the most popular brand stories are the company-centric tactical story and the customer-centric tactical story.

Company-Centric Tactical Stories

In the case of company-centric tactical stories, usually, the company creates brand value. The story develops by making the managers and employees as the principal characters: heroes and heroines. Still, customers remain as protagonists who want to consume the brand to achieve their personal identity goals by being part of the brand tribes. Often brand identity becomes customers' identity. The essence of company-centric tactical brand stories resides in the core of the positivistic brand paradigm, which perceives (Heding et al. 2016):

- Marketers own the brand by controlling the communications.
- Consumers are the recipients of brand messages with no or very little ability to control the brand communication.
- Marketers create brand equity with the ability to manipulate the brand communication, as brand is perceived as "a manipulable artefact" (Hanby 1999, p. 12).

Virgin brand is a classic example, positioning the founder and the employees as the role model.

Case Study 4.2: Virgin Atlantic: 25 Years, Still Red Hot Featuring Relax by Frankie Goes to Hollywood

A busy city professional (financial industry executive) in a formal suit, jacket off, carrying a briefcase, exits a cab at the busy airport entrance in 1984, with an old large mobile. He walks into the airport, amongst the crowd of passengers and notices at a distance a female walking, wearing all red. Her entrance catches everyone's attention at the terminal, followed by high heels shot of multiple females, all wearing red. Everyone, including the airport police, notices them as they surround the pilot of the plane, who is caught by female passengers. In the end, one gentleman notices the attention received by the pilot from female passengers and says, "I need to change my job", and a younger passenger, who probably notices the all red stewardesses, replies to the other gentleman, "I need to change my ticket". The ad finishes with a zooming out shot of a Virgin Atlantic 747 with the slogan "Still red hot".

Reflective Questions

Watch this video and reflect on how brands tell company-centric tactical story through brand commercials or promotional videos.

1. Explain the significance of consumers' expressions: "I want to change my ticket" and "I want to change my job".
2. What are their relevance to company-centric tactical story?

Note Virgin Atlantic—25 Years, Still Red Hot Featuring Relax by Frankie Goes to Hollywood commercial is available on https://www.youtube.com/watch?v=FYQHDadIDxk.

Customer-Centric Tactical Stories

The customer-centric tactical stories portray customers as the hero or heroine of the story. The shift from company-centric to customer-centric tactical storytelling, mostly triggered by the advancement of digital technology and social media, is a new trend. Digital technology and social media have empowered all most everyone to tell stories and share those with the rest of the world. In customer-centric tactical storytelling, the brand value is co-created by brands and consumers. Brands with a passion for telling stories, dive into the customers' inner world and understand their life stories before crafting the stories customer want to hear. Finally, the brand shares the stories through various channels of communication, preferably social media platforms. These stories have the power to engage with the customers and create brand affinity. The customer-centric tactical story helps the customers to become heroes and clarifies the brand image. Often it also helps in explaining company mission to employees and defining brand identity so that employees can live brand values at work and can co-create brand stories with their customers. All though applicable to all kinds of brands, mainly the service brands use these types of brand stories as their product are mostly intangible, complex and perishable. In case of service, brand values to be sold to the employees first, which in turn help the customers to co-create brand experience and brand values. The concept of co-creation of brand value through brand engagement has been popular through the constructivist/interpretive brand paradigm, which suggests that brand is co-created by both marketers and consumers: this facilitates interaction between marketers and consumers (Heding et al. 2016). An ideal example is the commercial of Airbnb, which shows how a customer is telling brand stories and creating an emotional brand appeal (see Case Study 4.3).

Case Study 4.3: AirBnB: Never a Stranger

The ad starts with a woman next to a window in her AirBnB rented place as she does her internal monologue of her experience in Paris, being from New York. Her friends called this "crazy", as it was "someone else's house" not a hotel. We see all of her experiences, from Mexico, to Tokyo, Rio De Janeiro. Each city is a continuation of her experience of living in other people's homes, as she experiences life as if she was a local and not a stranger there. Other people's lives become her lives in each new place she visits where she says "you friends reminded me of my friends". The ad finishes with a line saying, "With over a million homes around the world, you're never a stranger". The last second is a picture of the AirBnB and its slogan, which the female voice recites, "AirBnB, belong anywhere". This commercial unveils the power of story, mainly when it is told by the consumers.

Reflective Questions:

1. Have you ever thought that one day your house, your flat and even your little room can be branded and your stories can be told by

people from all over the world? What does this tell about how branding is evolving and encompassing all aspects of our lives?

2. Can you find out three adverts that tell customer-centric tactical stories? What do these commercials have in common? Can you deduce some success criteria while comparing these adverts?

Note AirBnB—Never A Stranger commercial is available on: https://www.youtube.com/watch?v=s4WVhcXogGk.

Delivering Functional and Emotional Brand Values

The concept of brand has been originated as a differentiator of the products of one manufacturer from others (Gabay 2015). However, the contemporary thoughts have viewed brand beyond its visual attributes using interdisciplinary lenses and defined brand as a multi-dimensional construct, creating both ***functional*** and ***emotional*** values and consistently delivering them to meet customers' performance and psychological needs (de Chernatony and Dall'Olmo Riley 1998) (see Fig. 4.1).

The functional values relate to the features and benefits (mostly tangible) of products and services, which are the operational/functional aspects of branding: brands are guarantors of the quality (e.g. features and functional benefits) of the products and services promised by the manufacturers or service providers. The functional values of brands should be

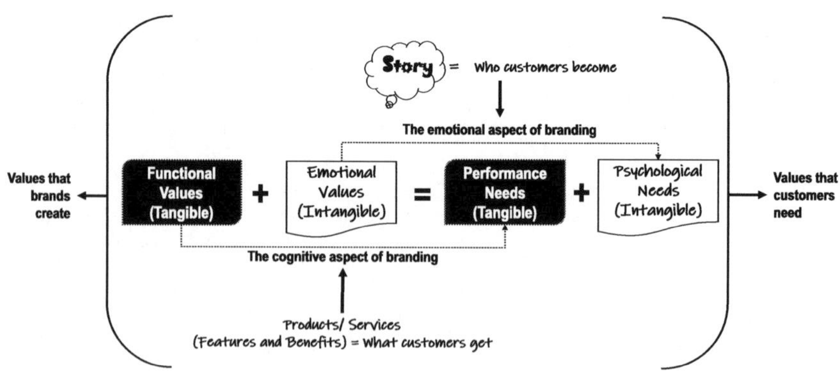

Fig. 4.1 A strong brand provides both functional and emotional values (*Source* Developed by author from de Chernatony and Dall'Olmo Riley 1998)

capable of meeting the performance needs of the consumers. In this case, the tactical brand-stories focus on the problems that customers are facing, and how brands can take care of these problems, leaving the customers free from anxiety.

On the other hand, the emotional values of brands relate to intangible benefits gained through the consumption of the products and services and are part of the psychological/symbolic aspects of branding. In this case, brands focus on emotional values and engage with customers to co-create the brand experience and brand meaning. The emotional brand values help consumers to fulfil their psychological needs. The brand stories focus on connecting with the customers emotionally, helping them discover their identity: who they are and the community or the tribe they belong to. de Chernatony and Dall'Olmo Riley (1998, p. 437) identified three essential ingredients that link to successful branding:

- Developing consumer-relevant values (intangible);
- Communicating these values effectively using symbols and designs (tangible);
- Consistently delivering the brand promises (functional: performance in terms of both tangible and intangible).

However, the best way to communicate these values are the brand stories (Aaker 2018; Jiwa 2019) because stories derive emotion (Krevolin 2016) and people first buy or decide with emotion and then justify with logic (Biesenbach 2018; Rodriguez 2020). Neuroscience's research has discovered that well-crafted stories can affect positively to releases oxytocin in customers' brain and help in the creation of emotional feeling and brand–consumers bonding (Stephens et al. 2010). Stories are the "emotional glue" (Krevolin 2016, p. 74) that connects the brands with the consumers. Brand stories need to fulfil some specific criteria to be effective. According to Aaker (2018), brand stories need to be intriguing, authentic and involving.

Intriguing

One of the purposes of marketing is to grab attention. In the age of information overload, as consumers receive thousands of messages every day, gaining attention becomes a priority. A brand may develop an excellent marketing campaign, but if it fails to grab attention, no one will get the brand message. Exposure to information should not be the target of brand communication. Instead, brand communications should attract both the sights and minds of the consumers so that the brand messages stick to their memory. For a story to be intriguing and stay in the memory of the consumers, Aaker (2018) asserts that stories should meet at least one of the seven criteria very strongly:

- Thought-provoking,
- Novel,
- Informative,
- Inspiring,
- Exceptionally relevant,
- Humorous, and
- Awe-inspiring.

In the age of social media with sharing trend, the intriguing story not only captures consumers' attention but also promote word of mouth communication.

Authentic

Authenticity and transparency are also crucial for successful brand stories. Brand stories need to be authentic to be able to make an impact. It should not appear as a manipulative endeavour to make sales. Authenticity helps the consumers to see behind the curtain. They can feel that brands have the courage to vulnerable through sharing the authentic self, which results in the formation of trust.

Authentic stories develop over time, and they are not fictions. For example, the strategic story of Shaukat Khanum Memorial Cancer Hospital is a true one, which tells how the loss that occurred in the life of Imran Khan, the former cricket legend of Pakistan (currently the Prime Minister), has brought hopes to millions of people in Pakistan. In February 1985, his mother, Shaukat Khanum, died after a battle with cancer. Imran was beside his mother while she was in the hospital, seeing her sufferings. During this time, he also witnessed the distress of other cancer patients and experienced the harsh reality: the scarcity of medical resources in Pakistan to treat cancer, which was costing lives. People with limited means affected him emotionally as he was wondering how the poor would cope with this disease.

After his mother had passed away, a belief that everyone, whether rich or poor, deserves an equal chance for treatment, sat him on a mission to raise fund for a hospital that will treat cancer patient for free. He launched the first fundraising appeal on 10 November 1989 during a cricket match between India and Pakistan at Lahore's Gaddafi Stadium. Soon it became a piece of global news. People could not believe; many even laughed at the idea of free cancer treatment. However, Imran Khan did not lose hope. In 1992, the Pakistan cricket team led by Imran Khan won the World Cup in Melbourne. Imran donated his prize money to the project, which dramatically made his appeal viral, raising £1.5 million in six weeks. The campaign continued. After five years of fundraising, Shaukat Khanum Memorial Cancer Hospital started its journey in 1994 as Pakistan's most prominent cancer charity. Till to date, the initiative of Imran Khan has dramatically changed the way cancer is treated in Pakistan with nationwide diagnostics centres, outreach screening clinics, two cancer hospitals in Lahore and Peshawar and 91 laboratory collection centres across 42 cities. It took many years for Imran Khan's Cancer Appeal to become an authentic story to which people are not only responding positively but also forming an affective attachment.

Involving

Involving brand stories draw audiences into the story according to narrative transportation theory (Mazzocco et al. 2010; Van Laer et al. 2014; Green and Brock 2002). Involving stories are compelling and create meaning in a way that results in "cognitive, emotional and/or behavioral response" (Aaker 2018, p. 12). In other words, the involving brand stories should have both cognitive and emotional elements to drive behavioural action. A cognition-driven involving story should nurture the intellectual curiosity of the consumers by giving them something to think and help in clarifying the brand message. Brands can incorporate the cognitive substance within the story by showing knowledge and understanding of the customers (Krevolin 2016). An emotion-driven brand story touches customers' hearts and precipitates their feelings (Aaker 2018).

Emotion drives people to cooperate and take action. As discussed in the previous chapter, neuroscience's research unveils that neurochemical oxytocin is produced in the brain bloodstream when people listen or watch emotional stories, which in turn, enhances peoples' disposition to trust others and cooperate (Garmston 2019). The classical theories of emotion assert that emotion is built-in within us and can be triggered. "The time-honored story of emotion goes something like this: We all have emotions built-in from birth. They are distinct, recognizable phenomena inside us.... We broadcast emotions into our faces by the way of smiles, frowns, scowls, and other characteristic expressions that anyone can easily recognize. Our voices reveal our emotions through laughter, shouts, and cries. Our body posture betrays our feelings with every gesture and slouch. Modern science has an account that fits this story, which I call the *classical view of emotion*" (Barrett 2017, p. x). Thus, emotional stories nurture our deeply rooted senses; and unlocks actions (Biesenbach 2018).

To conclude, storytelling is the language of brand-consumer conversations in the digital age of connectivity. Well-crafted brand stories—both strategic and tactical—connect with the consumers at a deeper level by nurturing their emotion. This chapter provides invaluable insights to practitioners, allowing them to create relevant stories, which foster conversations in the digital space and strengthen the bonding between the brands and the consumers.

References

Aaker, J. (2013). *Harnessing the Power of Stories*. Stanford Graduate School of Business. Available at: https://www.youtube.com/watch?v=9X0weDMh9C4. Accessed 12 Dec 2019.

Aaker, D. (2018). *Creating Signature Stories: Strategic Messaging That Energies, Persuades and Inspire*. New York: Morgan James Publishing.

Barrett, L. F. (2017). *How Emotions Are Made: The Secret Life of the Brain*. London: Pan Macmillan.

Bennet, A., & Royle, N. (2004). *An Introduction to Literature, Criticism and Theory*. Harlow, UK: Pearson Education Limited.

Berger, J. (2013). *Contagious: How to Build Word of Mouth in the Digital Age*. New York: Simon and Schuster.

Biesenbach, R. (2018). *Unleash the Power of Storytelling: Win Hearts, Change Minds, Get Results*. Orrington Ave Evanston: Eastlawn Media.

de Chernatony, L., & Dall'Olmo Riley, F. (1998). Defining a 'Brand': Beyond the Literature with Experts' Interpretations. *Journal of Marketing Management, 14*(5), 417–443.

Delgado-Ballester, E., & Fernández-Sabiote, E. (2016). "Once Upon a Brand": Storytelling Practices by Spanish Brands. *Spanish Journal of Marketing, 20*(2), 115–131.

Elliott, R., & Percy, L. (2007). *Strategic Brand Management*. New York: Oxford University Press.

Fog, K., Budtz, C., & Yakaboylu, B. (2005). *Storytelling—Branding in Practice*. Berlin, Heiddelberg: Springer-Verlag.

Gabay, J. (2015). *Brand Psychology: Consumer Perceptions, Corporate Reputations*. London: Kogan Page Limited.

Gallo, C. (2016). *The Storyteller's Secret: How TED Speakers and Inspirational Leaders Turn Their Passion into Performance*. London, UK: Macmillan.

Garmston, R. J. (2019). *The Astonishing Power of Storytelling: Leading, Teaching and Transforming in a New Way*. Thousand Oaks, CA: Corwin.

Green, M. C., & Brock, T. C. (2002). In the Mind's Eye: Transportation-Imagery Model of Narrative Persuasion. In M. C. Green, J. J. Strange, & T. C. Brock (Eds.), *Narrative Impact: Social and Cognitive Foundations* (pp. 315–341). Mahwah, NJ: Lawrence Erlbaum.

Hanby, T. (1999). Brands Dead or Alive. *Journal of Market Research Society, 41*(1), 9–19.

Heding, T., Knudtzen, C., & Bjerre, M. (2016). *Brand Management: Research, Theory, and Practice*. Oxon: Routledge.

Jiwa, B. (2019). *The Right Story: A Brief Guide to Changing the World*. Australia: Perceptive Press. https://www.amazon.co.uk/Right-Story-brief-guide-changing/dp/0994432828/ref=sr_1_1?dchild=1&keywords=The+Right+Story%3A+A+Brief+Guide+to+Changing+the+World&qid=1602796025&s=books&sr=1-1.

Krevolin, R. (2016). *The Hook: How to Share Your Brand's Unique Story to Engage Customers, Boost Sales, and Achieve Heartfelt Success*. Wayne: The Career Press Inc.

Mazzocco, P. J., Green, M. C., Sasota, J. A., & Jones, N. W. (2010). This Story Is Not for Everyone: Transportability and Narrative Persuasion. *Social Psychological and Personality Science, 1*(4), 361–368.

McCraty, R. (2015). *Heart-Brain Neurodynamics: The Making of Emotions*. In Issues of the Heart: The Neuropsychotherapist special issue, M. Dahlitz & G. Hall, Editor 2015 (pp. 76–110). Dahlitz Media: Brisbane.

Muñiz, A. M., Jr., & O'Guinn, T. C. (2001, March). Brand community. *Journal of Consumer Research, 27*, 412–431.

Rodriguez, M. (2020). *Brand Storytelling: Put Customers at the Heart of Your Brand Story*. London: Kogan Page.

Sinek, S. (2009). *Start with Why: How Great Leaders Inspire Everyone to Take Action*. London: Penguin.

Stephens, G. J., Silbert, L. J., & Hasson, U. (2010). Speaker–Listener Neural Coupling Underlies Successful Communication. *PNAS, 107*(32), 14425–14430.

Stern, B. (1994). Authenticity and the Textual Persona: Post Modern Paradoxes in Advertising Narrative. *International Journal of Research in Marketing, 11*(4), 387–400.

Van Laer, T., Ruyter, K. D., Vsconti, L. M., & Wetzels, M. (2014). The Extended Transportation-Imagery Model: A Meta-Analysis of the Antecedents and Consequences of Consumers' Narrative Transportation. *Journal of Consumer Research, 40*(5), 797–817.

Walter, E., & Gioglio, J. (2019). *The Laws of Brand Storytelling: Win—And Keep—Your Customers' Hearts and Mind*. New York: McGraw-Hill.

Walvis, T. (2010). *Branding with Brains: The Science of Getting Customers to Choose Your Company*. Harlow: Pearson Education Ltd.

Woodside, A. G., Sood, S., & Miller, K. (2008). When Consumers and Brands Talk: Storytelling Theory and Research in Psychology and Marketing. *Psychology and Marketing, 25*(2): 97–145.

CHAPTER 5

Character and Plot: Narrative Structure and the Art of Archetype Enactment

Abstract Characters and plots are at the heart of storytelling, bringing life to stories and stories to life. Plots and archetypes within the brand story help in transporting customers into the story world, binding them with emotional glue. Used appropriately, they affect customers' sympathy and love for the protagonists. This chapter, drawing on interdisciplinary literature, introduces a conceptual model and explains the critical elements of story: narrative structure, characterisation, plots including seven basic plots and widely used Hero's Journey framework. While the academic researchers can find pathways to further their research, the practitioners can leverage theoretical insights in creating and evaluating brand stories with an opportunity to transform the practices of brand storytelling and business narratives.

Keywords Narrative structure · Characters · Plots · Hero's Journey · Heroic transformation · Story themes

People are natural storytellers (Gottschall 2012; Rodriguez 2020) and respond to stories. However, the question is, are they good storytellers? (Rodriguez 2020). Stories happen always but not the good stories that attract our attention and influence our hearts and minds. Developing good stories and telling them compellingly require mastery of both art

S M A Moin, *Brand Storytelling in the Digital Age*,
https://doi.org/10.1007/978-3-030-59085-7_5

and science. The legendary screenwriting coach Robert McKee explained it well:

> From an instant to eternity, from the intracranial to the intergalactic, the life story of each and every character offers encyclopaedic possibilities. The mark of a master is to select only a few moments but give us a lifetime. (1997, p. 11)

Therefore, expert storytellers know how to deduct the boring things from life to make life more compelling to the listeners.

Towards an Interdisciplinary Conceptual Model

The interdisciplinary academic research mainly contributed towards divergent narrative theories and enriched the field of storytelling. There is however, very little effort to integrate theories. This gives an opportunity to contribute in the convergent narrative theories. Responding to this call, a conceptual model has been grounded from the interdisciplinary literature of storytelling (Fig. 5.1).

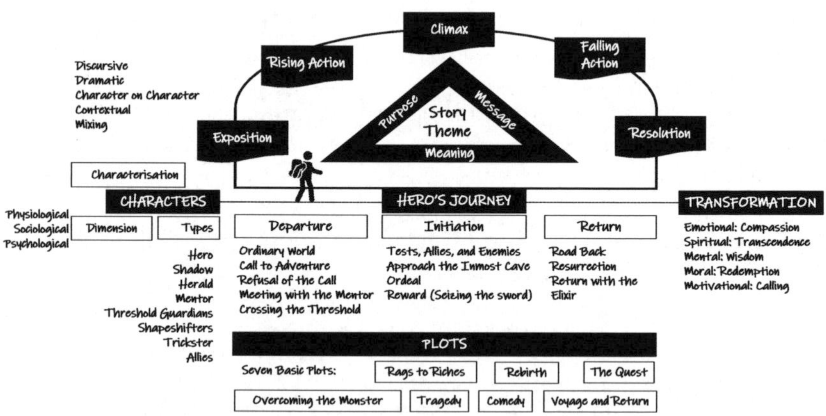

Fig. 5.1 A conceptual model for creating and evaluating stories (*Source* Developed from Campbell [1949], Wellek and Warren [1955], Kenney [1966], Pickering and Hoeper [1981], Card [1998], DiYanni [2001], Moscardo [2010], Allison and Smith [2015], and Allison and Goethals [2017])

Character and Characterisation

Characters are the essential elements that bring stories to life by bringing life into the stories: "In most from of narrative literature, character development is central to the story" (Chestek 2008, p. 142). In literary works, it is coined as fictional identities (DiYanni 2001), that "carry the readers from first to last page, making the readers care" (Reissenweber 2003, p. 26). Characters make the story relatable so that the readers can imagine themselves in the story, and the story becomes a reflection of their own life, which is explained well in the words of the renowned Hollywood screenwriter Robert McKee.

> Deep within the protagonist the audience recognizes a certain shared humanity.... But there's something about the character that strikes a chord. In that moment of recognition, the audience suddenly and instinctively wants the protagonist to achieve whatever it is that he desires. (McKee 1997, p. 141)

Allison and Goethals (2011) have identified several characteristics—smart, strong, caring, selfless, charismatic, resilient, reliable, and inspiring—that different characters within a story mimic to show their personalities and values, allowing the readers to understand them better. Card (1998) and Abrams (1999) posit that characters are defined by what they say, what they do, what they believe or what they stand for. Good writers know the art of projecting these values so well that the readers can easily understand the protagonist(s), the antagonist(s), and the supporting characters of the story. The characterisation is an art. Good writers also know how to use this art to bind readers with the character (e.g. protagonist) emotionally. The characters of a story become part of audiences' lives if done skilfully. For example, the lead character, Baker Bhai, developed by renowned Bengali novelist, Humayun Ahmed, in a Bengali drama "Kothao Keu Nei" meaning "There is no one anywhere",[1] conquered a position in the heart of the Bengali audiences. The national TV channel telecasted the drama serial for many months. Before the final episode, the novelist hinted a possible death sentence of the lead character, Baker Bhai. The audience could not accept this as Baker Bhai could win

[1] A brief description of this Bangladeshi TV Serial can be found here: https://en.wikipedia.org/wiki/Kothao_Keu_Nei.

a place within the heart of the viewers. There were huge processions countrywide, urging the novelist to change the plot so that the judge does not give a death sentence to Baker Bhai. Nonetheless, the novelist ended the serial with the death of the main character, and there was a massive demonstration throughout the country.

However, the writers should not manipulate the readers with too simplistic or too unrealistic (Card 1998) qualities of a character. The over-exaggeration can cause distrust and readers may disengage. While creating suspense and interest is a way to engage the readers, the writers need to provide proofs in support of the activities of the characters to keep the audience engaged. The narrative theories cover many aspects related to characters: character type (Tarigan 1984), characterisation (Kenney 1966), and the dimension of character (Wellek and Warren 1955).

Character Type

There are many characters in life, so in stories, as stories are reflections of lives. The following words of William Shakespeare—in Speech: "All the world's a stage"—make this point metaphorically:

> All the world's a stage,
> And all the men and women merely players;
> They have their exits and their entrances;
> And one man in his time plays many parts,
> His acts being seven ages.

Often they are also known as narrative archetype. Drawing on Megehee and Woodside (2010), Delgado-Ballester and Fernández-Sabiote (2016) have identified several characters such as siren, hero, antihero, creator, change master, powerbroker, wise old man, loyalist, mother of goodness, little trickster, and the enigma. Vogler (2007), Campbell (1949), and Jung (1959) have also mentioned about hero, shadow, herald, mentor, trickster, and allies. However, the widely used archetypes are as follows:

Hero

Hero is the principal character within a story. Usually, the hero is strong, competent, and display moral character and courage. Often they start week but through struggles they transform into a morally sound person.

Shadow

Shadow is the villain or antihero who usually breaks the ethical norms to achieve the evil objectives and directly stand in the way of the hero.

Herald

Herald represents the person(s) or event(s) that call for an adventure; particularly in the Hero's Journey plot.

Mentor

Mentor is the guide or helper who helps the hero in his or her transformation. In the brand story, the ideal role for a brand is the mentor.

Threshold Guardian

The gatekeepers who often block the roads for the hero to access to valuable person or resources.

Shape-Shifters

In some stories, shape-shifters are the ones who show two-faced characters.

Trickster

Trickster plays a similar role like a villain or work against the hero, also known as mischief-maker.

Allies

Like mentors, allies also help the hero to overcome the challenges and transform in the end.

However, Tarigan (1984) divides these wide ranges of characters into three main categories: the main character, secondary character, and supporting characters. The main character—also known as the hero or protagonist—of the story plays the most crucial role. The protagonist has a desire that raises the stake of the story. This stake also links with the moral of the story. The secondary character mostly relates to the main character, while the supporting characters help the story flow and incidentally engage with the principal and secondary characters.

Characterisation

Characterisation plays an essential role in the success of a story. Yasmin (2017) defined characterisation as an art of revealing characters in the story. It is a way of introducing the characters to the audiences/readers, helping them to form relationships with the living entities of the story. There are several ways of characterisation in the narrative literature: discursive, dramatic, character on character, contextual, and mixing method (Kenney 1966).

In discursive approaches, the authors narrate about the characters, thus introducing them to the readers. In the dramatic approach, characters introduce themselves through what they say and do. However, what others say about them defines the character in "character on character" method. When the surrounding verbal context introduces characters, it is known as the contextual method. In the mixing method, multiple methods institute the roles within the stories. One of the ways of bringing characters to life is to use several dimensions of the characters, helping readers/audiences relate with them better.

Dimensions of Characters

In the narrative literature, three significant dimensions of a character—physiological, sociological, and psychological—have been widely used (Wellek and Warren 1955). The vivid physical description of the characters using their sex, age, shape, size, height, colour, and facial appearance form the physiological dimension (Yasmin 2017). Characters can be vividly brought to life through their sociological dimension (Roucek and Warren 1963), which includes all aspects of their social lives including economic, political, and social; as well as the interrelationships between them (Wellek and Warren 1955). The psychological dimension is also a compelling way of unveiling the nature of the characters, which focus on the psychology of the actors (Bernhardt 1953). In general, the motivation, feeling and emotion define the psychological dimension of the character (Yasmin 2017). This also involves identifying character's unique qualities rather than the typical attributes, manifested through projecting the contrasting traits: "The best contrasts are so seamlessly sewn with the characterization that they're not easy to spot; they seep into the characterization. The reader should experience the tension, not be spotting contrasts like stop signs along the road" (Reissenweber 2003, p. 32).

The use of the physiological, social, and psychological dimensions of the characters help the readers or listeners not only to see the characters but also enter into their inner world. In his popular TED talk entitled as "Choice, Happiness and Spaghetti Sauce", Malcolm Gladwell masterfully used all these dimensions to vividly describe one of the lead characters of his story: "Howard's about this high, and he's round, and he's in his 60s. He has big huge glasses and thinning grey hair, and he has a kind of wonderful exuberance and vitality. He has a parrot, and he loves the opera, and he's a great aficionado of medieval history. By profession, he is a psychophysicist" (Karia 2015, p.18).

Desire-Stake

Another vital element of the story is the art of using a desire-stake dilemma. This can be used as part of characterisation. The readers/audiences need to conceptualise the desire of the main character, i.e. the hero or protagonist. This helps the readers put into the shoes of the protagonist and transport themselves into the story. Reissenweber (2003, p. 26) says: "Desire beats in the heart of every dimensional character." The protagonist should desperately want something, whether it is tangible or intangible. The writers should capture the inner desire of the protagonist and unveil it to the readers, as they are unlikely to follow a protagonist who does not have compelling goals to achieve and does not strive to achieve them. Passionate desire provides incredible mental strengths to hero/protagonist to set forth on a mission to defeat the dragons and cross all the roadblocks: s/he not only embarks on the adventure but also take the readers/audiences through the journey. However, the readers/audiences also want to know the level of stake or risk if the protagonist fails to achieve the goals (McKee 1997). These are the questions that tie the readers with the protagonist, following him/her everywhere.

The Story Plot

Like the characters within a story, the plot is also one of the most essential narrative elements. Sari (2017) has defined "plot" as a sequence of events through which characters navigate through the story. The designing of the plot is an art of selecting and sequencing the events "…to navigate through the dangerous terrain of story and when confronted by a dozen branching possibilities to choose the correct path. Plot is the writer's choice of events and their design in time. " (McKee 1997, p. 43). Thus, plots help the story move forward while taking the readers along the way, who keeps on asking what comes next with tons of curiosity in their eyes. In one hand plot should be designed in a way that keeps the readers engaged with the "major dramatic question" (Aaker and Chang 2009, p. 3). Good plots keep the readers wondering about the future events, as they cannot predict clearly how the things will unfold, but at the same time plots should not be entirely unbelievable for the readers. The effectiveness of story and storytelling—particularly raising curiosity and holding the interest of the readers—significantly depends on the creation and organisation of the plots.

Levels/Sequences Within a Plot

Pickering and Hoeper (1981) identified five sequences in designing good plots such as exposition, rising action, climax, falling action, and resolution.

The "exposition" marks the beginning of the story by setting the stage through introducing the character within time, place and relevant background information which tends to be a stable world for the protagonist with a desire to achieve something. It unveils the story setting, showing the place where the story starts or takes place. To write a good story, the writer must know the story world with clarity and should be specific rather than vague so that the readers can see the real world where the story occurs (McKee 1997).

As the "rising actions" begin, a series of incidents start making the world around character instable with the protagonist going through many conflicts (Chestek 2008). These conflicts raise the interest of the readers: they cannot wait to know what is going to unfold, eventually taking them to climax.

The "climax" is defined as the "moment of the greatest tension in a story" (Sari 2017, p. 86). At the climax, the protagonist faces the antagonist with the highest level of conflicts. This takes audiences at the peak of interest and curiosity. This is the moment when the story world is mostly unstable for the protagonist, but through the "falling actions" the stability start to regain and the tension gradually calming down, preparing the audience find the answer to the major dramatic question. The story, finally, ends with a "resolution". Often most of the story ends with a happy ending where "the protagonist can be able to solve the problem, defeat enemies, and find the true love and live happily ever after" (Sari 2017, p. 87).

Types of Plots

There are many ways plots can be designed. However, in the literature, the seven basic plots gained special attention (Booker 2004).

Rags to Riches

Rigs to riches plots make the classic underdog story where the protagonist becomes the best through coming from ashes, i.e. nowhere. Everyone ignore him/her at the being but due to some miraculous turnaround, the protagonist researches at the top. Marketers creatively leverage the brand story to elevate the customer (protagonist). A classic example of "Rags to Riches" is the American biographical drama film directed by Gabriele Muccino, which shows the life of Chris Gardner, a homeless salesman who managed to find his dream job and become rich.

Rebirth

A recovery story is one where the protagonist reinvents himself/herself or learn to see the world differently. Significant inner development takes place in the life of the protagonist. In the case of brand stories, brands need to play a vital role in transforming their customers. An example of "Rebirth" is "A Christmas Carol" where Ebenezer Scrooge, an elderly, transformed from a miser into a kinder person.

The Quest

The quest is an adventurous story where the protagonist after a long journey, finds a treasure or accomplishes something, e.g. finds someone lost or saves someone's life or fulfils a dream. The quest shows a progression or personal developmental journey of a protagonist after overcoming many obstacles and temptations along the way. The film, "Lord of the Rings", based on work of English writer John Ronald Reuel Tolkien, portraits "The Quest" plot.

Overcoming the Monster

In this classical "good versus bad story", the protagonist fight and defeat the evil force. In the conventional brand story using this plot, brands play the role of guide, helping the protagonists (consumers) overcome the monster (the big problem in life). A perfect example of "overcoming the monster" plot is "Star Wars".

Tragedy

Ending in a depressive way where the protagonist is taken over by the antagonist, the story with "tragedy" portrays the dark side of humanity, moral weakness, and deep suffering. This is a way of giving the message that will not be easily lost from the frame of the readers. One of Shakespeare's most popular and frequently performed plays, Romeo and Juliet is a classic example of tragedy, where nothing but the death of two young lovers reconciled their feuding relationships between the two families.

Comedy

Given the critical reality of life and the mundanity of the daily routine where we often behave like machines, "comedy" primarily brings some joys in our life by making us laugh. Offering people the gift of laughter is not an easy task, and comedy plays a vital role in delivering this task. The story usually ends with a happy ending, bringing some ease and relief in our lives. William Shakespeare's "A Midsummer Night's Dream" is a famous comedy. This plot, written about 1595–96, captures the events related to the marriage between Theseus, the Duke of Athens and Hippolyta, the former queen of the Amazons.

Voyage and Return

Very similar to "The Quest" plot, the "voyage and return" plots portray the transformation of a protagonist through a voyage where she learns to see life from a different perspective. The voyage gives the protagonist to interact with different people and live in different parts of the world, which change her worldview. So, she returns with invaluable experience and wisdom. "Gulliver's Travels" is an example of the "Voyage and Return".

The Hero's Journey

Another well-known plot is Campbell's (1949) Hero's Journey monomyth. This is widely used by both movies and brand commercials. Hero's Journey has got extensive attention in interdisciplinary research covering consumer research (Buchanan-Oliver and Seo 2012), destination marketing (Moin et al. 2020), and tourism (Robledo and Batle 2017). The popularity of Hero's Journey comes from its connection to human life at a deeper level as within all of us there lives a hero, seeking to embark on a journey for self-transformation (Robledo and Batle 2017).

> Underneath the frantic absorption in the pursuit of money, status, power, and pleasure (…) are, we all know, a sense of emptiness and a common human hunger to go deeper (…) each of us wants and needs to learn, if not "the meaning of life", then the meaning of our individual lives, so that we can find ways of living and being that are rich, empowered and authentic. (Pearson 1989, p. xii)

The popular movies such as The Lord of the Rings, Spiderman, Harry Potter, Matrix, Lion King, Star Wars have used the plots drawn on the Hero's Journey. Same is the case for many brand commercials such as "Nike: Choose go", "Coca-Cola: Thank your Christmas Hero", "Heineken: Champions League", which have used the essence of Hero's Journey. Campbell's (1949) Hero's Journey monomyth has seventeen stages, which are divided into three phases: Departure, Initiation, and Return. The departure represents a separation from the life of comfort zone into an unknown world, the initiation represents a process of transformation, and finally, the return represents the comeback of transformed person who is ready to make a social impact.

Hero's Journey, Phase 1: Departure

Stage 1: Initially, the hero lives in the ordinary world, which is his comfort zone. But at some point, s/he gets a "Call to the Adventure" to set forth on a journey into an unknown world.

Stage 2: But the hero is reluctant to step out of the comfort zone, s/he refuses to set forth for this transformational journey, known by "Refusal to the Call".

Stage 3: But there comes some extraordinary support, known as "Supernatural Aid".

Stage 4: The supernatural aid empowers the hero to take up the journey and "Cross the Threshold".

Stage 5: Once he gets into the "Belly of the Whale", there is no way to return, and so he makes a commitment for change.

Hero's Journey, Phase 2: Initiation

Stage 6: The second phase (Initiation) starts with "The Road of Trials" that presents the hero with a series of tests, tasks and challenges. Here failures play a significant role in his/her transformation.

Stage 7: At one stage, the hero experiences unconditional love while "Meeting with the Goddess".

Stage 8: There are temptations in the form of "Woman as Temptress" to deviate him from his mission.

Stage 9: Here comes the real mentor who has the power to empower him/her with the strengths to continue the quest—a stage, known as "Atonement with the Father".

Stage 10: This quest blesses the hero with the divine knowledge going through a metaphorical death, known as "Apotheosis (dies a physical death)": "the journey marks the death of a narrow, immature way of seeing the world and the birth of a wider, more enlightened way of viewing life" (Allison et al. 2019, p. 2).

Stage 11: But finally, he achieves his goal, known as "The Ultimate Boon".

Hero's Journey, Phase 3: Return

Stage 12: The transformed hero is reluctant to leave the joys found in the special (new) world, the stage known as "Refusal to Return".

Stage 13: But s/he manages to escape the boon through "Magic Flight".

Stage 14: For this s/he even needed the support of a rescuer, the stage is known as "Rescue from Without".

Stage 15: S/he then returns to his/her old world by "Crossing of the Return Threshold".

Stage 16: S/he is transformed as "Master of Two Worlds", achieving a balance between the material (outer) and spiritual (inner) world.

Stage 17: Finally, the hero is transformed with the gift of "Freedom to Live"—a condition where he learns to live without fear. Now, the hero has no regret of the past and no concern for the future; s/he lives with peace and freedom of his inner and outer world.

Case Study 5.1: Beautiful Bangladesh: Land of Stories

"Beautiful Bangladesh: Land of Stories" is a promotional video to attract tourism in Bangladesh. This is one of the top promotional destination brand videos that used most of the stages of the Hero's Journey template to promote the cultural heritage of Bangladesh.

Phase 1: Departure

It unfolds with a western young man taking a bath in a beautiful lake in the early morning. It seems that with a lovely smile on his face, he is preparing for a mission, which can be referred to "*Call to the Adventure*" (Stage 1) of the hero's journey. As the sun is rising, the man starts his journey with his backpack, walking through a wooden bridge in the Sundarbans forest area of Bangladesh as if he is "*Crossing the Threshold*" (Stage 4).

Phase 2: Initiation

On the way, he has a glance of the Royal Bengal Tiger in the Sundarbans forest while capturing pictures of the surroundings but survived "The Road of Trials" (Stage 6). Several deer playing in the woods caught his attention, and he has to sit down for a moment to feel this experience. Then he meets with a local man (mentor) who tells him stories about the area, possibly about the Sundarbans and the Royal Bengal Tiger and the way to survive while experiencing the Sundarbans—can be compared with "Meeting with the Goddess" (Stage 7) as Goddess is a metaphorical term.

In the next plot, he travels by an engine boat in the Passur river, passing through the Sundarbans forest. While reading the newspaper sitting in his bed, he looks through the window to watch the beautiful scenery of the Sundarbans, a clear sign of happiness is visible in his face. The voice-over—"Happiness needs no reason"—sparks the emotion. Then he boards on a small country boat, experiencing the life of the poor fishermen of Bangladesh and enjoying a meal with fresh fish cooked on the boat. The voice-over—"This is what you feel when you come here"—brings reality into the imagination of the viewers. Then he comes to a beautiful hilly area and gets up on the roof of a local bus, enjoying the adventurous journey with the local people as the bus drives through the narrow roads of the Chittagong Hill Tracts. The joy shining through this natural smile means that the unobstructed views of the beautiful nature from the roof of the bus while playing the guitar sitting in the middle of the local people are worth for taking such a risky ride (Stage 6—"The Road of Trials" continues). The voice-over—"Things that you will do, people that you will meet will keep on surprising you"—seems to have the power to invite the potential travellers on a hero's journey. The joy knows no bounds as he is served with a big grilled-lobster during boat ride in a local lake in the next plot. Then he comes to Cox's Bazar, the longest sea beach of the world, where he runs in the unbroken beach and enjoys his freedom. On the way he joins with the local folk singers, dressing in the local costumes. Then he enjoys riding cow cart and finds a little girl who invites him into their house. While living in their house, he has exceptional experience of catching a cock bird with a young girl and her brother. He then participates in the Cox's Bazar water festival, a game played between boys and girls, throwing water to each other. A further challenge was to clean his teeth using tradition toothbrush, which he learns from a local old man. Although entirely new to him, he seemed to be fascinated by this experience. Back in the river, he now experiences timber rafting through riding on it. The next plot brings him to Ahsan Manzil in the banks of Buriganga River in Dhaka (the capital of Bangladesh), the official residential palace and seat of the Nawab of Dhaka. The voice-over, "your mind is a traveller, now your heart be the tourist guide" sparks curiosity in the minds of the potential tourists. The experience of old Dhaka is not complete without testing Bakarkhani (traditional biscuit), so the man was found enjoying it with a cup of tea in a stall. Then, wearing the national dress, he comes to Shaheed Minar (a national monument in Dhaka, established to commemorate heroes who were killed during the Bengali Language Movement demonstrations of 1952 in then East Pakistan), paying marks of respect with a bouquet of local flowers.

Now is the time to enjoy beautiful leaf flute played by a manual tricycle rickshaw driver of Bangladesh. What an experience of exploring a country and its people! This is followed by the experience of getting his beard shaved by a local barber sitting under the sky, an event in the lives of the ordinary people who can't afford to go to a proper salon. It is not over: through a local bus, he then goes to another hilly area and enjoys the beautiful peacock dance by a group of tribal girls with wonders in his eyes. "*Explore the land of surprises*"—the voice-over encourages him to continue his mission. This brings him to Srimongal tea garden, where he enjoys a cup of tea freshly sourced from the garden. While taking tea, he also enjoys the dance by the local girls. The voice-over "*You will find warmth you will be looking for all your life*" sets the emotional tone. He then plays Kabaddi (a national sports of Bangladesh) with the local people. The voice-over—"*Here everyone has a story to tell*"—fascinates him to be a guest of a local family. Living with the local village family and enjoying their hospitality, he experiences the life of the ordinary man living in the villages of Bangladesh. The househusband drying the hair of the guest with his own hands tells the story of love and affection these poor people can extend to strangers.

The man also experiences Katha Stitching by the female members of the family. Thus, the voice-over—"*So when you leave, you can leave with stories that you can treasure, friends that will last a lifetime*" seems to be a perfect example in inviting the potential tourist on a hero's journey.

Next, he plays cricket with the local village boys and flies sky lantern at night. In the "*Initiation*" phase all these unforgettable experiences transform a western man with the power and ability to live in an eastern country, which is culturally enriched particularly for its people who live with stories and celebrates hospitality (Stage 11: *The Ultimate Boon*).

Phase 3: Return

In the last plot, the man was walking back through the isle of the crop field but very slowly as if he is reluctant to leave this new world—*Refusal to Return* (Stage 12). However, the little girl with whom he has some unforgettable memories comes from his back, offering him a flower bouquet and a letter—possibly he was waiting for this moment. Experiencing this pure love for humanity makes him smile for the last time, which enables him to catch the *Magic Flight* (Stage 13) to return into his own world with experience of living in the east. Now, he has the knowledge of both worlds (Stage 16: *Master of Two Worlds*)—the east and the west and to live an extraordinary life (Stage 17: Freedom to Live).

Reflective Questions

1. Watch the promotional video, "Beautiful Bangladesh - Land of Stories" and critically analyse the characterisation and designing of the plots within the video.
2. What does the western hero signify in this eastern promotional video?

Heroic Transformation

Some of the most important reasons behind the popularity of Hero's Journey is embedded in the transformation that the protagonist goes through (Allison et al. 2019) and its relevance in our lives. We all are heroes in our little world of fantasy, and the power of imagination gives human beings the wings to fly in a fictional reality.

> everyone is a hero in birth, where he undergoes a tremendous psychological as well as physical transformation, from the condition of a little water creature living in a realm of amniotic fluid into an air-breathing mammal. (Rank 1909, p. 153)

Hero's Journey often helps us turn our fictional reality into objective reality through our heroic transformation. Good writers know how to show the heroic transformation, which allows them to connect with their readers at a deeper level, inviting them to a transformational journey and putting themselves into the shoes of the protagonist. They bring the shadow of our life into the canvas where the challenges we face and the roadblocks we encounter let us grow into an enlightened person. The heroic transformational literature mainly discusses six types of heroic transformation: one being physical leading to transmutation and the rest of the five being psychological transformation, leading to enlightenment (Allison and Smith 2015; Allison and Goethals 2017; Allison et al. 2019). Table 5.1 briefly describes five types of psychological transformation.

The storytellers and brand marketers need to consider these transformations while developing the brand stories and focus on how the products and brands can tell stories that show the customers (protagonists) going through the respective transformations that are aligned with the brand values. Particularly, this can be of great interest for the destination and tourism marketers as tourism in the current days are not limited

Table 5.1 The five types of heroic transformation

Types of transformation	*Refers to/involves*	*Known as*
Emotional transformation	Changes of the heart through which people grow empathy for others	Compassion
Spiritual transformation	Changes in belief systems	Transcendence
Mental transformation	Intellectual growth	Wisdom
Moral transformation	A dramatic shift from immorality to morality	Redemption
Motivational transformation	A complete shift in the purpose of life	Calling

Source Adapted from Allison et al. (2019), Allison and Smith (2015), Dik et al. (2017)

to escaping from the mundanity of routine life rather seeking the meaning of life as we travel (Robledo and Batle 2017).

The Story Themes and Transfer of Meaning and Message

Good stories also contain message wrapped within them. Themes are used in conveying the moral of the story (Chestek 2008). The storywriters use a wide range of themes—love, death, quest, adventure, revenge, rivalry, temptation, and good versus evil—to develop their accounts.

In the case of brand stories, the lessons sent through stories play a crucial role in promoting brand's purpose, values, and message, which covey the brand meaning and play a significant role in connecting with the target audience.

In summary, to develop compelling brand stories, the practitioners need to understand the narrative theories well with particular focus on the art of characterisation and developing the plots. Together, the plots and characters bring life to stories, showing a vivid picture of customers' inner world. With an interdisciplinary conceptual model, this chapter brings together the essential ingredients that can help in the development of compelling stories, thus, contribute to the convergent theories of storytelling.

References

Aaker, J., & Chang, V. (2009). How to Tell a Story (A), Case No. M323A (19 p.). Stanford Graduate School of Business. Available at: https://www.gsb.stanford.edu/faculty-research/case-studies/how-tell-story. Accessed 1 Dec 2019.

Abrams, M. H. (1999). *A Glossary of Literary Terms* (7th ed.). Boston, Massachusetts: Heinle & Heinle.

Allison, S. T., & Goethals, G. R. (2011). *Heroes: What They Do and Why We Need Them*. Oxford: Oxford University Press.

Allison, S. T., & Goethals, G. R. (2017). The Hero's Transformation. In S. T. Allison, G. R. Goethals, & R. M. Kramer (Eds.), *Handbook of Heroism and Heroic Leadership*. New York, NY: Routledge.

Allison, S. T., Goethals, G. R., Marrinan, A. R., Parker, O. M., Spyrou, S. P., & Stein, M. (2019, March). The Metamorphosis of the Hero: Principles, Processes, and Purpose. *Frontiers in Psychology, 10*, 1–14.

Allison, S. T., & Smith, G. (2015). *Reel Heroes & Villains*. Richmond, VA: Agile Writer Press.

Bernhardt, K. S. (1953). *Practical Psychology*. New York, London and Canada: McGraw-Hill Book Company Inc. https://archive.org/details/in.ernet.dli.2015.188585/mode/2up.

Booker, C. (2004). *The Seven Basic Plots: Why We Tell Stories*. London: Bloomsbury.

Buchanan-Oliver, M., & Seo, Y. (2012). Play as Co-created Narrative in Computer Game Consumption: The Hero's Journey in Watercraft III. *Journal of Consumer Behaviour, 11*, 423–431.

Campbell, J. (1949). *The Hero with a Thousand Faces*. Princeton, NJ: Princeton University Press.

Card, O. S. (1998). *Character and Viewpoint*. Cincinnati, OH: Writer's Digest Books.

Chestek, K. D. (2008). The Plot Thickens: The Appellate Brief as Story. *The Journal of the Legal Writing Institute, 14*, 127–169.

Delgado-Ballester, E., & Fernández-Sabiote, E. (2016). "Once Upon a Brand": Storytelling Practices by Spanish Brands. *Spanish Journal of Marketing, 20*(2), 115–131.

Dik, B. J., Shimizu, A. B., & O'Connor, W. (2017). Career Development and a Sense of Calling: Contexts for Heroism. In S. T. Allison, G. R. Goethals, & R. M. Kramer (Eds.), *Handbook of Heroism and Heroic Leadership*. NY: Routledge.

DiYanni, R. (2001). *Literature Reading Fiction, Poetry, and Drama*. New York: McGraw-Hill Book Company Inc.

Gottschall, J. (2012). *The Storytelling Animal: How Stories Make Us Human*. New York: Mariner.

Jung, C. G. (1959). The Archetypes and the Collective Unconscious. In H. Read, M. Fordham, & G. Adler (Eds.), *Collected Works* (Vol. 9, Part 1). Princeton, NJ: Princeton University Press (Originally published in 1916).

Karia, A. (2015). *TED Talks Storytelling: 23 Storytelling Techniques from the Best TED Talks*. Great Britain: Amazon.com Inc.

Kenney, W. (1966). *How to Analyze Fiction*. New York: Monarch Press.

McKee, R. (1997). *Story: Style, Structure, Substance, and the Principles of Screenwriting*. New York: HarperCollins.

Megehee, C. M., & Woodside, A. G. (2010). Creating Visual Narrative Art for Decoding Stories That Consumers and Brands Tell. *Psychology & Marketing, 27*(6), 603–622.

Moin, S. M. A., Hosany, S., & O'Brien, J. (2020). Storytelling in Destination Brands' Promotional Videos. *Tourism Management Perspective, 34*(100639), 1–12.

Moscardo, G. M. (2010). The Shaping of Tourist Experience: The Importance of Stories and Themes. In M. Morgan, P. Lugosi, & J. R. B. Ritchie (Eds.), *The Tourism and Leisure Experience: Consumer and Managerial Perspectives* (pp. 43–58). Bristol: Channel View Publications.

Pearson, C. (1989). *The Hero Within: Six Archetypes We Live by*. San Francisco, CA: Harper and Row.

Pickering, J. H., & Hoeper, J. D. (1981). *Concise Companion to Literature*. New York: Macmillan.

Rank, O. (1909). *Der Mythus von der Geburt des Helden*. Berlin: Franz Deuticke.

Reissenweber, B. (2003). Character: Casting Shadows. In A. Steele (Ed.), *Writing Fiction*. New York: Bloomsbury.

Robledo, M. A., & Batle, J. (2017). Transformational Tourism as a Hero's Journey. *Current Issues in Tourism, 20*(16), 1736–1748.

Rodriguez, M. (2020). *Brand Storytelling: Put Customers at the Heart of Your Brand Story*. London: Kogan Page.

Roucek, J. S., & Warren, R. L. (1963). *Sociology: An Introduction*. Totowa, NJ: Littlefields, Adams, and Co Paterson.

Sari, L. P. U. (2017). The Analysis of Characters and Plot in Draanen's Flipped. In G. A. G. Sosiowati & N. L. N. S. Malini (Eds.), *English Prose Analysis: From Theories to Practices* (1st ed., pp. 81–112). Bali: CAKRA Press.

Tarigan, H. G. (1984). *Prinsip-Prinsip Dasar Sastra*. Bandung: Angkasa Bandung.

Vogler, C. (2007). *The Writer's Journey: Mythic Structure for Writers*. Studio City, CA: Michael Wieise Productions.

Wellek, R., & Warren, A. (1955). *The Theory of Literature*. London: Lowe & Brydone Ltd.

Yasmin, A. R. (2017). The Analysis of the Main Character in Doyle's "The Adventures of Sherlock Holmes: The Boscombe Valley Mystery." In G. A. G. Sosiowati & N. L. N. S. Malini (Eds.), *English Prose Analysis: From Theories to Practices* (1st ed., pp. 81–112). Bali: CAKRA Press.

CHAPTER 6

Conclusion: The Future of Storytelling

Abstract Brand storytelling is at the heart of brand strategy. In the era of hyper-connectedness, it is more about brand–consumer conversations where although marketers are in the driving seats, customers are controlling the navigation. This chapter invites the opportunity for new research by triggering interest in the future of brand storytelling shaped by AI, VI, AR and big data. Experts predict a creative renaissance: ancient art will meet modern technologies and transform the way brands and consumers converse. Although the future is an unknown, the potential success depends upon how brands become authentic and infuse emotion in an AI-driven world through creating superior stories that promote humanity and resonate with their customers.

Keywords Brand storytelling · Creative renaissance · Brand-consumer conversations · Ad to Art · AI-driven world

Storytelling is inextricably linked to human evolution in many ways. Corn (2012) says "Story, as it turns out, was crucial to our evolution – more so than opposable thumbs. Opposable thumbs let us hang on; story told us what to hang to" (p. 1). As "human memory is story-based" (Schank 1999, p. 12), storytelling has helped us evolve using the intelligence passed by our ancestors : around the fire at night, our ancestors shared

S M A Moin, *Brand Storytelling in the Digital Age*,
https://doi.org/10.1007/978-3-030-59085-7_6

how they had survived themselves from adversities in the form of stories. We also imagine the future in the form of stories and prepare for it (Corn 2012).

From Ancient Art to Contemporary Marketing Science

The advancement of neuroscience reveals that storytelling has the power to release certain hormones in our brain, which increases our disposition and positively influence our attitude to cooperate (Rodriguez 2020). Marketers have tapped into the power of storytelling and eventually the ancient art of storytelling has evolved into contemporary marketing science with its incredible power to use emotion, cognition, and data intelligently. Seth Godin said: "Marketing is no longer about the stuff that you make, but about the stories you tell" (Cohen 2011). Stories have the power to win hearts, change minds, and deliver results (Biesenbach 2018). Storytelling is highly effective in communicating brand values, brand meaning and promoting brand differentiation (Delgado-Ballester and Fernández-Sabiote 2016). Herskovitz and Crystal (2010) proposed that in comparison to traditional marketing, storytelling is far more effective in promoting brand values. Storytelling helps in providing brands with a personality and brings brands to life (Delgado-Ballester and Fernández-Sabiote 2016), thus affecting brand attitude and purchase intention (Chiu et al. 2012) through fostering strong brand connection (Escalas 2004; Herskovitz and Crystal 2010). The role of storytelling in marketing is no longer limited to advertising. Instead, it is playing a pivotal role in the overall brand management strategy (Delgado-Ballester and Fernández-Sabiote 2016).

Shift in Mindset

Although marketing has always used stories, the evolution of brand storytelling has helped marketers in shifting their focus from a product-centric mindset to a customer-centric mindset. Conceptually, a product is made in the factory, whereas a brand is customers' perception about what the product can do (Walter and Gioglio 2019). Product-centric approach tends to convince customers that a particular product is the best mostly using marketing rhetoric and emotional manipulation where brands work as symbols of quality. The product-centric mindset considers customers as logical creatures (rational being) who evaluate products through complex analyses against a set of criteria. The customer-centric mindset takes a more humanistic approach, viewing customers as emotional creatures whose hearts are moved by stories infused with emotion. Marketing in the modern era of connectivity is no longer about convincing the customers about product superiority using statistics, facts and logics as research found that people buy with emotion and justify their decision after that with logic (Rodriguez 2020; Nanton and Dicks 2013; McKee and Gerace 2018; Krevolin 2016). In the changing digital landscape, brand storytelling is shifting the focus from brands and products to customers. The success mostly depends on the congruence between the values brand stories promote and the values customers admire and live in their day-to-day lives. Brands need to demonstrate empathetic awareness about customers' everyday life: the challenges they are facing; the desires and aspirations they are living with, the dreams they are pursuing and so on. These are the essence of brand storytelling in the post-advertising era instead of bragging about the product supremacy. What matters most is not what the brands tell about their products and services rather what customers perceive and believe about the brands and share their message with others.

Shift in Marketing and Brand Storytelling in the Digital Age

In the age of hyper-connectivity driven by social medial and digital transformation (Krevolin 2016), marketing is changing its discourse. Traditionally, marketers were in full control of creating and communicating the message. However, in the contemporary world, the power base is shifting. Although marketers are in the driving seat, the customers are navigating and creating meaning. The engagement and interaction between "consumers and consumers" and "consumers and brands" have transformed the traditional marketing game from playing "bowling" to "pinball" (Henning-Thurau et al. 2013). The traditional bowling game of marketing is compared with the broadcast model and are predictable as brand owners play an active role and tend to control all aspects of marketing communications. However, in a sharing economy through digital transformation, all industries are witnessing a transformational change. The companies that are adapting to these changes and leveraging creativity are surviving and growing whether they own strategic assets or not. The largest movie house, Netflix, owns no cinema; the most significant software ventures, Apple and Google, do not write apps; and famous media owner, Facebook, creates no content (Haque 2019). In the same way, marketing is evolving to play pinball wizardry, in a social media mediated dynamic environment where storytelling fosters collaborative co-creation of marketing contents between marketers and consumers (Singh and Sonnenburg 2012). The pinball wizardry game is about less controllable, peer-to-peer distributed, user-generated content, which aligns with the contextual change driven by the rapid advancement of digital technology and proliferation of social media in all aspects of our lives.

> In an always-on consumer world, the role of marketing needs to change from a batch of process of sequential campaigns into a trading room monitoring and engaging with the ebb and flow of conversation happening in the digital space context. It is, therefore, not just about storytelling anymore (which is self-contained unit of beginning, middle and end that has already occurred), but about timeless, ever evolving brand narratives that you must create and control. (Krevolin 2016, p. 16)

The Mysterious Future of Brand Storytelling

While creating opportunities for marketers to engage with the consumers, the new technologies, enhanced connectivity, and consumer empowerment in the new digital landscape bring tremendous challenges for the marketers. If user-generated messages spread falsehoods then brands have to build a convincing counter story, which often takes huge investment. Again, a small mistake by brands will have detrimental effect on the brand image. A song by Canadian singer, Dave Caroll, on YouTube[1] in 2009 (20,134,269 views as of 11 July 2020) made global news, costing United Airlines millions of dollars while shattering their brand reputation. It took United Airlines fortune to regain their brand image. Nonetheless, consumer empowerment makes the companies accountable, keeping them on track. If companies are creative, authentic and care for their customers, they will eventually do better: authenticity beats falsehood. Having faith

[1] United Breaks Guitars, available at: https://www.youtube.com/watch?v=5YGc4zOqozo (accessed on 11 July 2020).

in this moral value, Amazon.com to pioneer an online customer review culture, which helped the company to grow.

Creative Renaissance

This digital landscape enriched with enormous online tools, tactics, and techniques to create and co-create customer-generated stories, has already started a creative renaissance driven by storified branding and marketing communication. Where the classical model of brand communication invested the majority of their budgets on buying the distribution channel to create awareness, the social-media-driven free digital canvas can save companies an enormous amount.

> But in the world where thousands, maybe millions, share stories they love, the balance reverses: Tomorrow's story-driven marketers will invest the balance of their budgets in creating stories and a declining share in distributing them. This envisions a brilliant future for creatives. (McKee and Gerace 2018, p. 220)

Thus, there will not only be a shift from investing in the distribution channels to the development of the creative but also a shift in the way brands–consumers converse. The ancient art (storytelling) meeting with contemporary technologies (AI, VR, AR) will radically transform brand storytelling through creating an *artistic science* that will use both art (storytelling) and science (new media, new technologies, big data and so on), empowering marketers and customers to co-create compelling and creative brand stories. The *artistic science* will tend to be created where facts (data) meet with the fiction (art), and brands connect with customers' hearts and minds, nurturing the human spirit.

Ad to Art

In this new era of imagination, creativity, and innovation, many brands whose stories will not resonate with their customers will be irrelevant and lost. However, brands—that will put customers at the heart of everything they do and quest for creative renaissance through empowering their customers and employees to co-create marketing aesthetics—will flourish, marking a shift from ad to art. An example, as cited in the previous chapter, is "Lifebuoy Help a Child Reach 5—Tree of Life"[2] commercial that has harnessed the power storytelling using both science and art. The advert has used authentic characters, plots, real settings and statics of children deaths. The main protagonist in the story is a mother, living through love and loss, who represents all the mothers in a village in India whose children tragically die before reaching the age of five. The commercial shows the transformation of the mother (protagonist) with an invaluable lesson: washing hands can save the lives of many children. When the audiences fully transport themselves into the story, the brand appears as a helpful aid (mentor)—not at as a hero—to support mothers to clean their hands, telling how Lifebuoy saved many lives through their campaign. With no expense in buying the distribution channel, the brand could reach 11,536,299 views as of 11 July 2020.

Information to Imagination

We are also living in the age of information and imagination with a shift towards the latter. The power of information-driven by big data is fuelling our imagination, allowing the marketers to enter into the inner world of the customers. The resultant effects will continue to foster creativity and will drive innovation. As we are moving more into the imagination age, creativity is becoming a threshold competency rather than a competitive advantage. The new media and the range of powerful tools used within it will create a new fictional reality through harnessing the power of storytelling where customers will become the fictional protagonist in their world of fantasy. In this fictional reality, creative marketers will empower their brand tribes to unleash the genius inside them: letting them fly with their minds and navigate with their heart. There will be a creative revolution of brand–consumer engagement mediated by AI, VI and AR. The brands that will co-create meaning in the life of their customers will break the clutter and continue to triumph.

In the AI-driven world, while the future of storytelling is somewhat mysterious in the wake of the fastest pace of technological changes and no prediction guarantees how the tomorrows will continue to unfold, the author takes the position of an optimist and can sense a new era of brand storytelling revolution in the "post-advertising world" (McKee and

[2] Lifebuoy Help a Child Reach 5—Tree of Life, available at: https://www.youtube.com/watch?v=GCwgKFttQ7M (accessed on 11 July 2020).

Gerace 2018). While programmers will be writing computer cou. marketers will be busy with emotional coding and cognitive programming to craft stories that will win their consumers hearts and minds. Brand storytelling in the future will create momentum at the intersection of narrative art, modern technologies, and humanity, as Steve Jobs said: "It is in Apple's DNA that technology alone is not enough—it's technology married with liberal arts, married with the humanities, that yields us the results that make our heart sing" (Lehrer 2011: online).

The recent COVID-19 pandemic taught us humanity once again. In the new dawn, brand stories that will attract attention, infuse emotion, nurture humanity through using emotional and social intelligence will be able to create music in a world full of noise. These are the stories that will find the melody in the heart of their customer and shape the discourse brand communication.

However, questions remain as a source of inspiration for new research:

- In an AI-driven world, where many customers like to live in the fictional reality created by AR and VR, how are the creative marketers going to control the pinball game of marketing?
- How are the tomorrow's marketers going to infuse emotion and remain authentic while most of the things going to be machine-driven?
- How is the nature of brand storytelling going to change in the wake of on-going digital transformation?
- Will there be more paradigm shifts in the way brands going to tell stories in the future?

References

Biesenbach, R. (2018). *Unleash the Power of Storytelling: Win Hearts, Change Minds, Get Results*. Orrington Ave Evanston: Eastlawn Media.

Chiu, H. C., Hsieh, Y. C., & Kuo, Y. C. (2012). How to Align Your Brand Stories with Your Products. *Journal of Retailing, 88*(2), 262–275.

Cohen, H. (2011). *Seth Godin: 7 Truths at the Heart of Marketing (& How to Use Them)*. Heidi Cohen Actionable Marketing Guide. Available at: https://heidicohen.com/seth-godin-7-truths-at-the-heart-of-marketing-how-to-use-them/. Accessed 11 July 2020.

Corn, L. (2012). *Wired for Story: The Writer's Guide to Using Brain Science to Hook Readers from the Very First Sentence*. Berkeley: Ten Speed Press.

Delgado-Ballester, E., & Fernández-Sabiote, E. (2016). "Once Upon a Brand": Storytelling Practices by Spanish Brands. *Spanish Journal of Marketing, 20*(2), 115–131.

Escalas, J. E. (2004). Narrative Processing: Building Consumer Connections to Brands. *Journal of Consumer Psychology, 14*(1&2), 168–179.

Haque, E. (2019). *Digital Transformation Through Cloud Computing*. London: Enel Publication.

Henning-Thurau, H., Hofacker, C. F., & Bloching, B. (2013). Marketing the Pinball Way: Understanding How Social Media Change the Generation of Value for Consumers and Companies. *Journal of Interactive Marketing, 27*, 237–241.

Herskovitz, S., & Crystal, M. (2010). The Essential Brand Persona: Storytelling and Branding. *Journal of Business Strategy, 31*(3), 21–28.

Krevolin, R. (2016). *The Hook: How to Share Your Brand's Unique Story to Engage Customers, Boost Sales, and Achieve Heartfelt Success*. Wayne: The Career Press Inc.

Lehrer, J. (2011). Steve Jobs: "Technology Alone Is Not Enough", The New Yorker. Available at: https://www.newyorker.com/news/news-desk/steve-jobs-technology-alone-is-not-enough. Accessed 11 July 2011.

McKee, R., & Gerace, T. (2018). *Storynomics: Story-Driven Marketing in the Post-Advertising World*. York: Methuen.

Nanton, N., & Dicks, J. (2013). *Story Selling: Hollywood Secret Revealed How to Sell Without Selling*. Florida: Celebrity Press.

Rodriguez, M. (2020). *Brand Storytelling: Put Customers at the Heart of Your Brand Story*. London: Kogan Page.

Schank, R. C. (1999). *Dynamic Memory Revisited*. Cambridge: Cambridge University Press.

Singh, S., & Sonnenburg, S. (2012). Brand Performance in Social Media. *Journal of Interactive Marketing, 26*, 189–197.

Walter, E., & Gioglio, J. (2019). *The Laws of Brand Storytelling: Win—And Keep—Your Customers' Hearts and Mind*. New York: McGraw-Hill.

Index

S M A Moin, *Brand Storytelling in the Digital Age*,
https://doi.org/10.1007/978-3-030-59085-7